the OTHER JOURNAL

the OTHER JOURNAL

EVIL

An Intersection of Theology and Culture

presented by The Seattle School of Theology & Psychology

Copyright © 2012 *The Other Journal*. All rights reserved. Except for brief quotations in critical publications or reviews, no part of this publication may be reproduced in any manner without prior written permission from the publisher.

Cascade Books
An Imprint of Wipf and Stock Publishers
199 W. 8th Ave., Suite 3
Eugene, OR 97401
www.wipfandstock.com

ISSN 1933-7957
ISBN 13: 978-1-62032-596-4

Scripture quotations marked (ESV) are from The Holy Bible, English Standard Version® (ESV®), copyright © 2001 by Crossway, a publishing ministry of Good News Publishers. Used by permission. All rights reserved.

Scripture quotations marked (KJV) are taken from the Holy Bible, King James Version, Cambridge, 1769.

Scripture quotations marked (NIV) are taken from THE HOLY BIBLE, NEW INTERNATIONAL VERSION®, NIV® Copyright © 1973, 1978, 1984, 2011 by Biblica, Inc.™ Used by permission. All rights reserved worldwide.

Scripture quotations marked (TNIV) are taken from the HOLY BIBLE, TODAY'S NEW INTERNATIONAL VERSION®. Copyright © 2001, 2005 by Biblica®. Used by permission of Biblica®. All rights reserved worldwide.

Scripture quotations marked (RSV) are taken from Revised Standard Version of the Bible, copyright 1952 [2nd edition, 1971] by the Division of Christian Education of the National Council of the Churches of Christ in the United States of America. Used by permission. All rights reserved.

Scripture quotations marked (NRSV) are taken from New Revised Standard Version Bible, copyright 1989, Division of Christian Education of the National Council of the Churches of Christ in the United States of America. Used by permission. All rights reserved.

Manufactured in the U.S.A.

The Other Journal is based at The Seattle School of Theology & Psychology.

THE OTHER JOURNAL

Dan Rhodes :: Editor-in-Chief
Andrew David :: Managing Editor
Tom Ryan :: Executive Editor
Chris Keller :: Founding Editor
Jon Stanley :: Theology Editor
Brandy Daniels :: Assistant Theology Editor
David Kline :: Assistant Theology Editor

Allison Backous: Creative Writing Editor
John Totten :: Music and Film Reviews Editor
Ian Knippel :: Cinematographer
Jev Forsberg :: Intern
Sarah Perez :: Intern
Nathaniel T. Rogers :: Intern

EDITORIAL ADVISORY BOARD

Brian Bantum
Daniel Bell Jr.
Jason Byassee
William T. Cavanaugh
Pam Cochran
David Dark
Dwight Friesen
Amy Laura Hall

Peter Heltzel
Paula Huston
Fr. Emmanuel Katongole
Jeffrey Keuss
Ron Kuipers
D. Stephen Long
Charles Marsh
Charles Mathewes

Eugene McCarraher
Brian McLaren
Alison Milbank
John Milbank
Debra Rienstra
Luci Shaw
James K. A. Smith
Graham Ward

SUBSCRIPTIONS

The Other Journal (ISSN: 1933-7957) is published twice a year at the annual rates listed below.
USA Individuals: 1 year $30.00
USA Institutions: 1 year $40.00
International Individuals & Institutions: 1 year $40.00

CONTACT INFORMATION

Send all submissions and queries to submissions@theotherjournal.com or to *The Other Journal* at The Seattle School of Theology and Psychology, 2501 Elliott Avenue, Seattle, WA, 98121

Subscriptions may be ordered online at www.theotherjournal.com/subscriptions.

Subscription e-mail: subscriptions@theotherjournal.com
Advertising e-mail: info@theotherjournal.com
Phone: 206-876-6142
Website: www.theotherjournal.com

Contents

Letter from the Editors ix

1. Tillers of the Ground 1
   Poem by Kali Wagner

2. Overcoming Lamech: Lament as Antidote to Violence 3
   Essay by Branson Parler

3. Working through the Trauma of Evil: An Interview with Richard Kearney 7
   Interview by Ronald A. Kuipers

4. The Banal Road to Perdition:
   Cliché, Political Failure, and What the Tea Party Can Teach Us 15
   Essay by David Kline and Dan Rhodes

5. The Killer in Me Is the Killer in You: An Interview with Richard Beck 27
   Interview by Chris Keller

6. The Terrible and Sublime Liturgy:
   A Meditation on Evil, Scapegoats, and Beauty 35
   Essay by Agustín Maes

7. Burning Dog 47
   Fiction by Mark Fleming

8. Evil Is What Humans Do: An Interview with Christian Wiman 53
   Interview by Allison Backous

9   Open Your Eyes Wide: The Generous Vision of Marilynne Robinson 56
    Review by Rebecca Martin

10 Bleakness and Richness: Christopher Nolan on Human Nature 61
    Essay by Lauren Wilford

11 We the Village 70
    Fiction by Chad Gusler

12 Randomness and Assurance: Does Everything Happen for a Reason? 75
    Essay by Gregory A. Boyd

13 Thoughts on African American Theology and Suffering as Moral Evil 86
    Essay by Anthony B. Pinn

14 Evil, the New Atheism, and the God of the Trinity 94
    Essay by Jacob H. Friesenhahn

15 Race, Criminality, and the Divine Occupation:
    An Interview with J. Kameron Carter 102
    Interview by David Kline

16 Religious Activism, the Living Wage Movement, and Occupy Wall Street:
    An Interview with C. Melissa Snarr 111
    Interview by Brandy Daniels

17 Bloodline to Bethlehem: A Review of John Piper's *Bloodlines* 118
    Review by Brian Bantum

18 A Sense of Place: Flannery O'Connor and the Local Church 124
    Essay by Andrew W. E. Carlson

19 O for a Thousand Tongues to Mutter 129
    Poem by Jennifer Strange

    Contributors 131

Letter from the Editors

In his poem "God's Grandeur," Gerard Manley Hopkins famously wrote that "The world is charged with the grandeur of God. / It will flame out, like shining from shook foil;" and yet on a daily basis—in our Facebook feeds, our newspapers and magazines, our own lives—we are confronted with a world that seems charged with the crackling force of pent-up rage and selfish desire. It is a fallen place rife with suffering, oppression, and violence, a land of tsunamis and earthquakes, genocide and crime sprees. As Hopkins later writes, "All is seared with trade; bleared, smeared with toil; / And wears man's smudge and shares man's smell."

Hopkins speaks of a world where the celestial shine of shook foil infiltrates the muck of humankind. There is a sense, however, in which we can't exactly set down the coordinates of that phosphorous glint of sparking light. We can't always know how and where the mysterious grandeur of God is at work, changing lives and transforming our world. But what about the smudge and smell of man? We are surrounded on all sides by brokenness and hurt and pain, yet we have difficulty spotting its source. We see the effects of evil, yet we rarely grasp its true nature and breadth.

This issue of *The Other Journal* aims to address the topic of evil, both with regard to its obvious manifestations and its haunting opacity. At times our contributors lament the presence of evil and at times they call us to work against it. At times they analyze the Christian response to evil, critiquing it and offering some correctives, and at times they merely try to bring evil's more insidious or systemic forms to light. These essays, interviews, poems, and short stories resist easy definitions and explication. They suggest that evil is not always as easy to name as we Christians might think and that we may even, at times, be its willing and unwilling accomplices.

In Agustín Maes's essay "The Terrible and Sublime Liturgy," he suggests that "by traveling with the scapegoat into the wilderness it is possible to glimpse the ineffable truth." It is our hope that by surrounding ourselves with all this ambiguity, by wandering into the wilderness, we may see a bit clearer. Evil may remain obscure, but perhaps we might be better positioned to glimpse its presence in ourselves and others, to strike out against its effects, and as Andrew W. E. Carlson says in the final essay of this issue—perhaps evoking Hopkins—to "worship a God who breaks into all the corners of reality."

—Andrew David, Tom Ryan, and Dan Rhodes

1 Tillers of the Ground

by KALI WAGNER

And Adam knew Eve his wife; and she conceived, and bare Cain . . . and his brother Abel. And Abel was a keeper of sheep, but Cain was a tiller of the ground.

—GENESIS 4:1–2

The dirt under her nails, in her finger creases,
smells like iron, tastes like salt.

Eve smooths the barren soil
like a restless baby's back,
tracing circles of hush-a-bye, be still
to earth's trembling veins
as Abel's blood soaks the ground,
spreading and staining

topsoil, sediment, clay,
the water and dirt in my own mother's palms.
Spinning, it spackles her face,
shrouds her skin.

She, too, became a potter
when her youngest child died.
Dusting the house in porcelain
as fine as Matthew's ashes
and burying the yard in sculptures:

A pregnant torso in the dogwood,
and in the bougainvillea,
three tiny hands
reaching out of the ground,
index fingers crumbling.

2 Overcoming Lamech: Lament as Antidote to Violence

by BRANSON PARLER

"I WANTED THEN, AS I do now, revenge for what happened. Bring me the head of Osama bin Laden," wrote *Washington Post* columnist Richard Cohen on September 8, 2009. Cohen was in lower Manhattan on 9/11 and isn't shy about acknowledging his desire for revenge. At the root of his foreign policy, he declared (with complete seriousness), was his desire to grab bin Laden "by the throat and tear out his Adam's apple."

Cohen's sentiment finds a counterpart in the early pages of Scripture. One of the first poems recorded in Genesis is Lamech's boast. Lamech revels in vengeful violence: "I have killed a man for wounding me, a young man for injuring me. If Cain is avenged seven times, then Lamech seventy-seven times" (Gen. 4:23–24 NIV).

My first impulse is to deride and reject everything for which Lamech and Cohen stand. Lamech's boast, after all, is specifically countered in Jesus's command to forgive seventy-seven times (Matt. 18:22). Nevertheless, I've often found that my arguments don't carry as much weight as I'd wish, with Christians and non-Christians alike. The violence and suffering of 9/11 stands out so strongly in people's minds that all my theological arguments—about our vain attempts at peace without eschatology, about Jesus as suffering servant, about the church as a new creation—seem to fall on deaf ears.

But perhaps I'm going about things wrong. What if my carefully crafted arguments against violence are less compelling than singing and giving voice to lament over the evil in the world? What if, as John Howard Yoder suggests, the ultimate source of violence goes deeper than any rationalization we give for violence?[1] What

---

1. Yoder, "A Theological Critique of Violence," in *The War of the Lamb: The Ethics of Nonviolence and Peacemaking* (Grand Rapids, MI: Brazos, 2009), 30.

if the antidote for Lamech is thus not argument but lament? Perhaps we are to sing the kinds of songs that Jesus himself sang as he suffered (see Matt. 27:46 and Mark 15:34). And although we often focus on the way biblical lament questions and complains to God, the writers of such laments also veer toward the vengeance seeking of Cohen, asking God to execute judgment upon their enemies.[2] So when confronted with evil and injustice, what can lament do for our feelings of revenge and grief?

Lament recognizes the deep roots of vengeful violence. Cain, the first murderer, recognizes that his fratricide will provoke the broader human community to respond in kind: "whoever finds me will kill me," he says (Gen. 4:14). This retaliatory reflex, notes Yoder, seems to be wired into humanity. Cohen himself alludes to this by confessing surprise at the intense desire for revenge that engulfed him on 9/11 and has persisted for years. If Christian pacifists don't also recognize this vengeful drive, they make a huge theological and tactical error. Rather than deploring the cry for vengeance and justice, Yoder argues that we must confess that there is something to the "deep demand of blood for blood," even as it is expressed in the violent war lust of Lamech. These biblical laments not only question God and express the heart of those who are suffering but also at times demand God to respond in kind to the persecutors.[3]

I understand that this makes Christian pacifists uncomfortable, but lament is unsettling. An analogy may help. Many Christians ignore lament entirely because they fear that questioning God is somehow sacrilegious. As a result, they reduce Christianity to a superficial, bubbly faith, suppressing rather than bringing into the open their genuine questions and doubts about God. Here's the rub: when we hear calls for retributive justice and retaliation, Jesus-following pacifists sometimes advocate the same kind of suppression. Would we scoff at those who try to enlighten us, who tell us we should not doubt or complain to God? Yes, and rightly so. Then we must see why, as Yoder suggests, we also cannot enlighten people out of their vengeful impulses.[4] That stripe of optimistic liberal pacifism was weighed and found wanting long ago.

Just as God is big enough to handle our questions, God can handle these expressions of anger and vengeance. And not only can God handle these expressions; God also wants to redeem them in a way that goes beyond both the dead end of retaliation and the suppressive pacifism that wants to pretend vengeful feelings don't exist.

---

2. See, for example, Psalms 3:7, 5:10, and 31:17–18.

3. For Yoder's discussion of this vengeful retaliatory reflex and our "deep demand of blood for blood," see "Theological Critique of Violence," 33 and 41; also see Yoder, "You Have It Coming: Good Punishment," in *The End of Sacrifice: The Capital Punishment Writings of John Howard Yoder*, ed. John C. Nugent (Scottdale, PA: Herald, 2011), 227–28. For an example of biblical lament that demands a response, see Psalm 137, which begins in lament and ends with a benediction for those who kill Babylon's babies as retribution for the cannibalism that took place at the siege of Jerusalem (see Lam. 4:10).

4. Yoder, "Theological Critique of Violence," 30.

As Yoder puts it, "the gospel is not about delegitimizing violence so much as about overcoming it."[5]

This overcoming happens, in part, through the act of lament itself. Laments are performance; they *do* something. They work on the singers in particular ways. Questions and doubts about God are placed in the context of songs addressed to God, folding the singers' doubt into a larger performance of faith. Likewise, by placing their cries for vengeance in songs addressed to God, the singers are displaced from bearing the weight of history or vengeance, which enables them to leave vengeance to God (Rom. 12:19).

Yet those who, like Lamech, act on their feelings of revenge must bear an eschatological burden; they *must* make history turn out right. Lamech's war cry perpetuates the illusion of control and the illusion that humans can ultimately make meaning out of evil and suffering. In contrast, lament is apocalyptic, revealing that only God can take human suffering and evil and work a resurrection out of it. When Jesus sings Psalm 22:1 on the cross, it is not a cry of defeat but a victory song. He has resisted the satanic temptation to make history turn out right, embracing the way of lament rather than Lamech.

When we read biblical laments christologically, we see that our retaliatory reflex is not ignored but overcome by naming Christ's suffering as *sacrifice*. Yoder contends that "If the phenomenon of violence is not rational . . . neither will its cure be rational. The cure will have to be something as primitive, as elemental, as the evil. . . . It will have to be sacrifice." Cohen likewise uses terms freighted with theological weight to describe what he wants: "I don't think I'm all that different from a whole lot of other Americans who would like to . . . get some satisfaction from all the blood that was shed at . . . the World Trade Center, the Pentagon and that field in Pennsylvania, and in Afghanistan the last eight years."[6] Christians need not avoid this sentiment but should instead underscore that Jesus, not our enemy, absorbs the punishment for wrongs done. Jesus, not our enemy, has paid it all.

Rather than suppressing or avoiding those laments that call for payment in kind, we ought to bring them into the open, acknowledge the intense pain and suffering of evils like 9/11, and then point to the blood of Jesus. The wall of hostility crumbles only through his cross. The book of Hebrews, argues Yoder, sees "the end of expiation for bloodshed, the end—not as abrogation but as fulfillment—of the arrangement announced in Genesis 9:6 ['whoever sheds human blood, by humans shall their blood be shed'] is the innocent death of the Son."[7] Christian pacifists should not be

---

5. Ibid., 33 and 41. Also see Yoder, "You Have It Coming," 227–28.

6. Yoder, "Theological Critique of Violence," 30; and "Richard Cohen Still Wants Revenge For 9/11," interview by Neal Conan, *Talk of the Nation*, NPR, September 10, 2009, http://www.npr.org/templates/story/story.php?storyId=112717615.

7. Yoder, "Against the Death Penalty," in *The End of Sacrifice*, 132–33.

squeamish about the curses of Torah, the bloodiness of the cross, or the wrath of God. Instead, we must sing more loudly than ever that "Jesus paid it all, all to him I owe," recognizing that precisely because *Jesus* paid it all, our enemies don't need to. Because we sing that "on the cross as Jesus died, the wrath of God was satisfied," we no longer seek revenge. We can instead endeavor to overcome evil with good (Rom. 12:21).[8] We do not ignore evil, violence, and injustice, but we name them, express our fury over them, and praise the Slain Lamb for taking "the punishment that brought us peace" on himself (Isa. 53:5). As followers of Jesus, our call is not to rationalize with Lamech but to outsing him.

---

8. See the following two hymns: Elvina M. Hall and John T. Grape, "Jesus Paid It All," http://www.hymnwiki.org/wiki/images/6/6c/Jesus_Paid_It_All.pdf; and Keith Getty and Stuart Townend, "In Christ Alone," http://www.gettymusic.com/ica.pdf.

3 Working through the Trauma of Evil: An Interview with Richard Kearney

by RONALD A. KUIPERS

IN THIS INTERVIEW, THE Irish philosopher Richard Kearney explores the human experience of evil and the role of the human imagination in responding to this evil. Kearney focuses on the healing steps people may take in order to "work through" traumatic experience, steps that include remembering, narrative retelling, and mourning. Such working through, he says, can turn melancholia to mourning, thus allowing those who have experienced suffering and loss to "give a future to their past" and, in so doing, to "go on."

The Other Journal (TOJ): In your latest book, *Anatheism*, you cite with approval the declaration Hannah Arendt made in 1945 when she said that "the problem of evil will be the fundamental question of post-war intellectual life in Europe." In her landmark work, *Eichmann in Jerusalem*, Arendt had the audacity to describe a certain kind of monstrous evil as somehow the product of banality. It seems that in listening carefully to testimony from Adolf Eichmann's trial and forthrightly describing what she heard, Arendt was engaged in the imaginative effort of "working through" (*durcharbeiten*) trauma, a process that you describe in *Strangers, Gods and Monsters*. Eichmann was a monster that she faced rather than attempted to slay, and because of this subtle difference, she dared to interpret Eichmann differently than his prosecutors; she was able to discern that Eichmann was, in her words, "not Iago."[1] He was not out to prove himself a villain but rather someone quite dull and ordinary, thoughtless rather than

---

1. See Kearney, *Anatheism: Returning to God After God* (New York, NY: Columbia University Press, 2011), 59; Arendt, "Nightmare and Flight," in *Essays in Understanding, 1930–1945* (New York, NY: Harcourt Brace, 1994), 134; Kearney, *Strangers, Gods and Monsters: Interpreting Otherness* (New York, NY: Routledge, 2003), 103–5; and Arendt, *Eichmann in Jerusalem: A Report on the Banality of Evil* (New York, NY: Penguin, 1994), 287.

stupid, someone who saw himself as little more than a cog in a larger bureaucratic machinery. Could you share your thoughts on Arendt's vision of evil?

Richard Kearney (RK): I'm quite partial to Arendt's analysis. One could argue that the style of her book was too dispassionate, because when she speaks of banality it can sound dismissive, as if the horrendous events of the Holocaust don't matter, which is untrue, both in terms of history and in terms of what Arendt intended. But I think she's right that identifying this evil as banal demystifies and demythologizes it and renders human beings responsible. It renders Eichmann himself responsible above all, and of course the Nazis. But it also reminds us that holocausts, genocides, and other forms of unspeakable horror can also occur elsewhere. No nation, race, or country is exempt. Why? Because even the most radical forms of evil are human.

This doesn't mean we are all equally responsible for Auschwitz. I'm not a Nazi, and I don't want a Jungian relativist to come along and say we're all Nazis and that we all carry the Nazi around inside of us. I don't think we are all Nazis, but it is still very humbling and humanizing to recall how many good and potentially good people were taken in by Hitler. And it's not only the Germans who have this in their DNA and who seem to love dictators. Look what's going on in Syria, Libya, Iran, Iraq, and North America—this tendency is potentially in every people.

When Eichmann was imprisoned during his trial, the jailer who looked after him was named Captain Less. Eichmann and this jailer talked a lot, and at one point, shortly before he died, Eichmann realized that Captain Less had children, and loved dogs, and had dreams, just like any of Eichmann's own next-door neighbors. And one senses that if Eichmann had realized this earlier, he would not have been able to kill Jews as he did. This suggests that murder is the death of imagination. What Eichmann lacked was empathic imagination; he was unable to imagine that the person beside him—that the person he was demonizing as a Jew, the person who he believed deserved to be killed in order to purify the German race—was actually someone just like him. That's banal. That's an everyday, simple kind of discovery.

Now, take a step back. We also run the risk of scapegoating and demonizing Eichmann. We run the risk of mythologizing him as this evil beast who was possessed by the devil, as this man who was part of the dark German race that mysteriously, inexplicably, and inscrutably performed a horror that no one can ever understand. The great thing about the Eichmann trial is that when he was brought back from Argentina for trial—an act that was denounced by the United Nations, the American government, and Argentina as an infraction on the sovereign rights of Argentina and the rights of Eichmann, and yet an act that was itself ethical—there were endless days of prosecution and defense, and all of these testimonies were told, these simple stories that showed the banality of the horror of evil.

Rivka Yoselevka tells her story during Eichmann's trial and it's so moving because it's so ordinary—it's ordinary in the sense that we are with her as she goes to the German guards who take away her child and murder her family. And so to recognize the banality of evil is to increase our sense of the horror, not to diminish it. If we mythologize it and demonize it, then we say that it has nothing to do with us, that it has nothing to do with humanity, and that it is inhuman. But the terrible thing about evil is that it is human. And it's more: evil is the absence of God, the absence of being, the absence of the good.

When we make divisions between the utterly pure and the utterly impure, that is one of the greatest sources of evil—that's where scapegoating comes from. At the same time, I do not endorse the relativity of evil and good. I am not saying that Eichmann is just like us. If someone took Rivka Yoselevka aside and suggested that she could be Eichmann and he could be Yoselevka, that she is good and evil and so is Eichmann, as if the only difference between the two is where they stand in relation to the jail bars, that would be false. Yoselevka is an innocent victim and Eichmann is an evil perpetrator of torture and genocide. They're not the same. But to recognize the banality of evil, even Eichmann's evil, is to recognize that this man, following orders in a daily everyday way, lacked the imagination and empathy to recognize that the people he was killing were not monsters but other human beings.

This brings us to the matter of how we deal with evil and work through its consequences. One of the ways that the Eichmann trial did this—as did the Bloody Sunday tribunal in Northern Ireland and the Truth and Reconciliation tribunals in South Africa and Rwanda—is that the perpetrators had to admit what they'd done and listen to the stories of the people who were persecuted and tortured. That process of working through trauma is not a cure, but it is nevertheless important for survivors to be heard and understood. Evil blocks the power to erase, to remember, and to imagine, and working through that trauma—whether it is through therapy, truth and reconciliation tribunals, psychoanalysis, confession, or writing—helps us to honor our debt to the dead and to give a voice to the voiceless, as Paul Ricoeur says. The Auschwitz survivor Primo Levi kept living for as long as he kept writing, testifying to the story so that it could be read and heard. And then, when he could write no more, he committed suicide. What kept him going, what kept him alive, was, as he put it, this elementary need to keep on telling the story so that it would never happen again.[2]

I think one of the great errors of killing Osama bin Laden was that America missed an opportunity to work through trauma. When the Serbian military leader Ratko Mladić was picked up in a little farmhouse—very much like Eichmann—and put on trial in The Hague, his victims got a chance to tell their stories. I'm a great fan

---

2. See the chapter "Conclusions," in Ricoeur, *Time and Narrative*, vol. 3 (Chicago, IL: University of Chicago Press, 1988); and Levi, *The Drowned and the Saved* (New York, NY: Summit Books, 1988).

of President Barack Obama, but if there was any possibility of bringing bin Laden back alive, it should have been taken, because in hearing his story and the stories of the survivors and the families of those people who died at his hands, something very important would have happened. It would have become impossible to scapegoat bin Laden. That's not to say he was not evil—he was evil and what he did was evil—but there's a banality about what he did. Human beings can do monstrous acts, and there is a danger in treating human monstrosity as so alien that it becomes a serpent or a dragon, that it becomes the beast.

Of course, that's exactly what bin Laden did. He didn't see Americans; he saw the Big Satan. He didn't see Jewish Israelis, Christian Israelis, Arab Israelis, or Muslim Israelis in Israel; he saw the Little Satan. And in that way, the Osama bin Laden versus George W. Bush showdown was characterized by mutual scapegoating. I'm not suggesting there's moral equity here—I'm on the side of America against bin Laden; I believe in democracy—but it was an error not to put him on trial as the Jews did with Eichmann. The trial of Eichmann in Jerusalem was an important example of moral integrity; it allowed the stories to be told, it allowed us to recognize the banality of evil, and it showed us that we could have done that too. We didn't do it—and I hope we would never do it—but we're human beings, and for better or for ill, members of humanity have been able to do that, are capable of doing it, and can do it again.

My uncle was a prisoner of war in a Japanese camp for five years, and for a time afterward he couldn't walk down a street in London if there was a Japanese person nearby. He had to walk away. Now, he was ashamed of this. He said that he tarred every Japanese person with the same brush because of the horrors he experienced at the hands of his captors. They tortured everyone in his camp, and he was one of only two survivors. His best friends were crucified on barbed wire. Worse things happened in Auschwitz, as you know, and terrible things have happened in Srebrenica and in Rwanda, and they're still going on today in Syria. These examples all show that the danger we must avoid is the vilification of others. If we refer to our victims as rodents or to the perpetrators of horrible acts as dragons, then in both cases—and they're very different cases, obviously—we have a tendency not to analyze and understand as best we can. As Baruch Spinoza said, when faced with something evil, do not despair, do not seek revenge, but try to understand.[3] When faced with evil, we must recognize that there is something there that we're meant to wrestle with and seek to understand, even if we never understand it fully. There's something irreducibly inscrutable about the worst kinds of radical evil, but we can't take the easy route and just dismiss such evil as monstrous. We can use the word *monstrous* to describe it, but only if we also recognize that the monstrous is human and that the monstrous can be banal: a man

---

3. See Spinoza, *Ethics*, trans. R. H. M. Elwes (1677; Project Gutenberg, 2009), part 5, proposition 38, http://www.gutenberg.org/files/3800/3800-h/3800-h.htm.

can be really nice to his children, read Shakespeare, listen to Beethoven, and then kill innocent people. That's the inscrutable enigma of evil, and it's an enigma we need to reckon with.

TOJ: That's how I understand Levi in the poem that begins *If This Is a Man*, where, in reference to the trauma of the Holocaust, he admonishes his readers to "meditate that this came about." That sentence jumps off the page at me because it suggests we have to stare evil down, to think again that this has happened. It suggests an ethical responsibility to avoid quick and easy answers. In both *Strangers, Gods and Monsters* and *On Stories* you discuss the importance of moving past a forgetful or amnesiac melancholy, through a transformative work of mourning, and to something like forgiveness. How does this transformative process work and what role does it play in terms of our experience of traumatic evil?[4]

RK: That's very tricky. I think Shakespeare's *Hamlet* offers a way to consider this. If a trauma is from an inexperienced experience, as is the case with Hamlet, then one often remains in amnesiac melancholy. Hamlet has been away in Wittenberg, and so he was not there when his father was murdered and he has not seen his father being buried. And so Hamlet's father comes back as a ghost because Hamlet hasn't processed or experienced the trauma. It's unfinished business for him—there's something rotten in the state of Denmark, there's something out of joint. Hamlet is caught in this melancholy state where he can do nothing for as long as he can't let go.

Hamlet clings to an illusion that his father was perfect: he goes to Gertrude's boudoir, holds up two pictures, and says, "Here is my father, your husband; he was like a god, like Hyperion. And here is my uncle Claudius, your new husband; he is a satyr."[5] Hamlet has this idea of the perfectly good father and the evil anti-father. Hamlet is told by his father, the dead king, to remember him, and so Hamlet wants to hear the story of his father, to know what happened so that he can remember, so that he can carry it on and tell the story himself. But Hamlet's father is forbidden to tell the story of something that happened but that has not been acknowledged, and so his father says, "But that I am forbid / To tell the secrets of my prison-house / I could a tale unfold whose lightest word / Would harrow up thy soul" (1.5.13–16).

Then, during the course of the play, particularly through his interactions with the gravedigger, Hamlet learns that his father was not so perfect, that it was Yorick, the poor lowly court jester, who had been his real father, looking after him, carrying him on his shoulders while his royal father had been involved in a war with

---

4. Levi, *If This Is a Man / The Truce* (London, UK: Abacus, 1987), 17; and see Kearney, *Strangers, Gods and Monsters*, ch. 7–8.

5. Paraphrase of *Hamlet*, ed. W. G. Clark and W. A. Wright (Oxford, UK: Clarendon, 1878), 1.2.140–41: "So excellent a king; that was, to this / Hyperion to a satyr . . ." References are to act, scene, and line.

Fortinbras's father; and he also learns during this same gravedigger scene that the two kings had fought a dual to the death on the very day Hamlet was born. He goes through this process where he learns that his father committed a sin as a youth that condemned him to hell, surrounded by sulfurous fumes. We are never told exactly what this crime is, but there are lots of hints and guesses throughout the play, and it is Hamlet's business to try to find out—"by indirections find directions out" (2.1.65). Finally, at the end of the play, as he is dying—as he dies to his illusions—Hamlet goes from melancholy to mourning. He lets go of everything, including his illusions about his father, and at that point he says to Horatio, "Absent thee from felicity awhile / . . . to tell my story" (5.2.330–332). It is as if Hamlet—the name of Shakespeare's own son was Hamnet—is telling Shakespeare the author and dramatist (alias Horatio) to tell his story by writing it down and telling it to us the audience! And then Fortinbras arrives at the end and says, "I have some rights of memory in this kingdom, / which now to claim vantage doth invite me" (5.2.373–374). Thus, memory and storytelling are retrieved. The suppression of the truth and the cover-ups of the crimes—both Claudius's crime and Hamlet's father's crime—which were symptoms of the ongoing revenge cycle, are brought to an end. And there's something crucially healing about Hamlet (thanks to Shakespeare) finding the right words for this enigma. Indeed, we all carry secrets with us and therefore we live in melancholy because, like Hamlet, we find it so difficult to let go of our cover-up illusions and idealized projections. It's only by reexperiencing the repressed experience—by confronting the secrets, the fears, the delusions—that we can go forward.

Now, if you take the example of the Holocaust trauma, as I do in *On Stories*, it's interesting that two important movies, *Shoah* by Claude Lanzmann and *Schindler's List* by Steven Spielberg, provide two different ways of telling the trauma. In *Shoah*, Lanzmann has people who still have memories of the Holocaust look at the camera and tell their stories. Many of the survivors had blocked those memories because that's how they survived: they became two people, they disassociated. Many of those who suffered in Auschwitz came back from the war and they never spoke again. That's a way of surviving; but to survive the survival, you've also got to take the next step, if you can, which is to tell the story. And there are two ways of doing that: you either tell the story directly, as some of them did in *Shoah*, or else you tell the story vicariously. One of the survivors of Schindler came up to me after a lecture I gave in Montreal and told me that she could never have done what some of her fellow survivors did in talking directly about their experiences in front of a camera (and indeed, some of the survivors who spoke to Lanzmann directly committed suicide, because it was just too much to bring back that memory). But the survivor who spoke with me said that by watching the movie *Schindler's List*, through the distance of an imaginary, fictionalized dramatic narrative (that was of course based on historical events), she was able to revisit the experience of the Holocaust and see herself go through that experience in a way that wasn't too much to bear. Through the detour of narrative imagination she was able to return to that inexperienced experience and reexperience it. She was thereby giving a future to her past, surviving her own survival, and living again to tell the tale.

Thus, there are different ways in which we try to work through an unspeakable evil. There can never be a literal reenactment—that would be like reliving it all over again—but by putting it into certain words, particularly in the form of a narrative, we can create enough distance from the past to properly work through it. And in that sense, we learn to survive the trauma. The trauma never goes away—trauma is the wound that silences us and paralyzes us; in Greek it is a wound that cannot be closed—but to survive a trauma is to learn to live with it.

TOJ: In *On Stories* you mention that Lanzmann was trying to resist the temptation to put something so sensitive, something that a person can't make sense of, within a narrative frame.[6] However, as you note, some of the people in the Lanzmann film were revictimized or retraumatized by the project, which might explain why some of them killed themselves after participating in it. It seems that you are suggesting that by creating some distance from their traumatic experiences and enabling survivors to see it through a story that wasn't their own, Spielberg's approach allows them to experience their trauma vicariously, and so work through it in a way that avoids reopening the trauma. And that is revelatory to me because before you made this comparison, I would probably have assumed that Lanzmann was taking the higher road.

RK: Until I met that woman in Montreal and heard her give her version of the story, I thought Lanzmann was right too—even when he said that catharsis in the Aristotelian sense of purging traumatizing affects (*pathemata*) is impossible when it comes to the Holocaust. But now I believe it is in fact possible. Viewing one's experience through the mediation of narrative gives that person a certain distance so that what Aristotle calls the purgation of the emotions of pity and fear by pity and fear can occur.[7] The Holocaust survivor I met in Montreal was able to identify with herself because the self was another self, dramatized by somebody else, played by an actor. She experienced pity by virtue of being able to identify with *herself as another*, and she also experienced cathartic fear, which is a kind of detachment, a kind of distance, that enabled her to be not completely fused with the other. It's that dialectic of being able to pity and empathize with a victim while at the same time standing back and

---

6. See Kearney, *On Stories* (London, UK: Routledge, 2002), 50–51.
7. See Aristotle, *Poetics*, 1449b, 25ff.

trying to understand why this is going on. That dialectic of the two is what enables it to work.

In *On Stories* I talk about Helen Bamber who is one of the founders of Amnesty International and one of the first counselors who met with the survivors of the Bergen-Belsen concentration camp. She describes how when she first visited the inmates, all she could do was listen. She said that people would either be totally silent, mute, lying on their beds motionless, or they would sit up and suddenly start speaking, speaking, speaking. As she put it, it was like a vomit that they were emitting. And the Greek word *katharsis* is again relevant here as it is used for the letting of blood, vomiting, menstruation, and the purging of toxic fluid. Bamber tells of how the survivors would see a dramatic presentation of Nazis barging in on a typical Jewish family, brutalizing the mother, taking the children, beating up the father, and so on. This scene would be repeated, and the audience would watch this scene, and they would identify with the characters. But they also realized that that was then and this is now. And that's the only way to deal with trauma. You must live the moment of the trauma, because as an inexperienced experience it never goes away. It comes back as a gap, an absence, a ghosting in repetitive flashbacks. It comes back in physiological reactions and allergies and phobias and acting out and so on. In trauma, there is no sense that that was then and this is now. But the drama, or the dramatizing of their experience, enabled these survivors to watch themselves suffering. They were able to find empathy for and with themselves and to experience a certain healing detachment from the evil itself. Once they had reenacted, however basically, some kind of shared narrative of their horror, they could walk out the doors of Bergen-Belsen. And that seems to me to be extremely telling as a way of overcoming evil. We tell what cannot be told in order to live on. Or as Samuel Beckett's *Unnamable* narrator puts it in the final sentence of that book: "I can't go on, I'll go on."[8]

---

8. See Beckett, *Three Novels: Molloy, Malone Dies, the Unnamable* (New York, NY: Grove, 2009).

4 The Banal Road to Perdition: Cliché, Political Failure, and What the Tea Party Can Teach Us

by DAVID KLINE & DAN RHODES

WE REMEMBER THE FIRST time we encountered the argument that the simplicity of PowerPoint presentations actually facilitated the US decision to enter into Iraq.[1] This strategy runs something like the strategy employed by third graders when turning in their first report for school: make sure it has a really nice cover and binding. If it looks good, it likely is good. Presenting such themes as "shock and awe," "surgical precision," and "minor resistance," there seemed to be no need to consider any complications. After all, in the slides it seemed so simple, so clear, so common sense. We chuckled when we read the argument, because while it is obviously far-fetched, it also seems to possess some kernel of truth—it's true that we were told how easy the offensive was going to be, how we could accomplish the plan with little to no collateral damage. Our guess is that if any of us would have known how difficult, complex, and messy these wars were to be, we likely would have chosen an alternative direction. So there does seem to be something to the notion that a false sense of simplicity can lead us into making decisions we wouldn't normally make.

In 1961, Adolf Eichmann, a Nazi officer who was designated by Reinhard Heydrich to orchestrate and oversee the mass deportation of Jews to ghettos and death camps during World War II, was captured in South America and extradited to Israel. For his role in the mass slaughter of hundreds of thousands of Jews, Gypsies, homosexuals, disabled persons, and other ethnic and political minority groups, Eichmann faced charges of war crimes and crimes against humanity. Hannah Arendt famously

---

1. For a description of some of these arguments see Elisabeth Bumiller, "We Have Met the Enemy and He Is PowerPoint," *New York Times*, April 26, 2010, http://www.nytimes.com/2010/04/27/world/27powerpoint.html.

covered the trial for the *New Yorker*, providing us with her interpretation of both the events and the people involved.[2] The Eichmann one finds in her account, however, is not the monster one would anticipate. Arendt's Eichmann is not an evil genius. He lacks the magnetism or ingenuity of a Hollywood villain, and he seems unable to offer more than simple slogans and quips to justify his actions. He's a bit boring, a bit mundane and simple. Arendt notes,

> . . . the same stock phrases and self-invented clichés (when he did succeed in constructing a sentence of his own, he repeated it until it became a cliché) each time he referred to an incident or event of importance to him. Whether writing his memoirs in Argentina or in Jerusalem, whether speaking to the police examiner or to the court, what he said was always the same, expressed in the same words. The longer one listened to him, the more obvious it became that his inability to speak was closely connected with an inability to think, namely, to think from the standpoint of somebody else. No communication was possible with him, not because he lied but because he was surrounded by the most reliable of all safeguards against the words and the presence of others, and hence against reality as such.[3]

These stock phrases and clichés functioned for the dull Eichmann as a means of navigating the actions required by his job. Any contradiction or crisis of thought arising from his internal sense of morality and his conduct was resolved by recourse to a slogan or catchphrase that would once again inspire confidence.

In other words, Arendt shows us that these clichés functioned for Eichmann as an impassioned means of surmounting what would have otherwise been profound and deep contradictions in his thinking and actions. These phrases operated in the stead of critical thought, conversation, patience, and spiritual struggle and thus allowed him to move on with his work. In fact, Eichmann "had at his disposal a different elating cliché for each period of his life and each of his activities."[4] Surmounting the complexities and inconsistencies he encountered in following the Nazi party line merely meant discovering the will to continue on, and this, it seemed, only depended upon finding the right cliché. Repeated often enough and with enough passion, the phrase itself resolved the contradiction for Eichmann, whose elation in using such phrases only betrayed his dependence upon them for maintaining a grasp on his distorted sense of reality. In this way, Eichmann was able to esteem himself the friend and benefactor of Jews even as he was orchestrating their mass deportation and arranging for them to be herded into death camps.

2. See Arendt, *Eichmann in Jerusalem: A Report on the Banality of Evil* (New York, NY: Penguin, 1994).
3. Ibid., 49.
4. Ibid., 53.

Although Eichmann's trial was more an exercise of judicial theater than anything else, Arendt's analysis of him seems pertinent to our contemporary political context. The current spectacle that passes for political engagement, we think, most vividly appears in the chorus of clichés and stock phrases that have become the running drivel of our politicians. More theater than argument, more competing brand advertisement than real disagreement, the political debates of our country have become a consumer product on par with the Super Bowl or *American Idol*. In a culture that thrives on the production of packaged commodities to make our lives simpler, political engagement (having solutions to the problems society faces as opposed to arguments about the types of lives we want to live) has become a catalog of talking points and catchy slogans that merely provide an illusion of having a true understanding of things.[5] To this extent, these political catchphrases function, much as they did for Eichmann, as a means of moving beyond complications and deep issues without really engaging them.

Our point here is not to equate our current political speak with the evils of Nazism but simply to point to the role that cliché played in facilitating the participation of an ordinary and simple person in forms of social evil much greater and more disastrous than anything seen before. To be human is to be political, and to be political is to find ourselves wrestling at times with contradiction. The fact that people will disagree about how to solve the problems we now face is not the problem. What we think is most problematic about the current state of political discourse is the degree to which both sides are increasingly dependent upon recycling clichés and stock phrases (under the auspices of talking points) in order to appear *as if* they have real answers to the problems of political life.[6] The absurdity of such posturing is obvious. The contradictions of modern life cannot be resolved simply by the party lines

5. The Marxist theorist Guy Debord points out that in a society that has reduced all human relations into objects of capitalist production, all social reality is mediated by images, or representations of truth, and these images predetermine the needs and desires of society's subjects by making subjectivity itself an image to be reproduced. Late capitalist society is now a spectacle *in toto*. When economic production is the end-all goal of society, the illusion of truth (the image) becomes truth itself because there now exists nothing beyond the spectacle's perpetual reproduction of itself. In this way, for the politician in late capitalist society, the image of truth, or the cliché, is the limit to political speech: "The society which rests on modern industry is not accidentally or superficially spectacular, it is fundamentally *spectaclist*. In the spectacle, which is the image of the ruling economy, the goal is nothing, development everything. The spectacle aims at nothing other than itself." See Debord, *Society of the Spectacle* (Detroit, MI: Black and Red, 1983), sec. 14; also see sec. 4 and 14.

6. As Karl Barth states with regard to slogans, catchwords, or clichés, "The slogan is not designed to teach, instruct, or convince the hearer or reader. It aims to exert a drum-roll influence on people by awakening associations, engendering ideas and the associated feelings, and issuing marching orders. It does not initiate or permit any reflection or discussion, but it hammers home an axiom that must precede and underlie any possible reflection and discussion." Hence, as he continues, "Slogans are simply vents with whose help ideologies surface and in the form of loud whistles call for *general* applause and acknowledgment." See Barth, *Church Dogmatics*, vol. 4, pt. 4, *The Christian Life: Lecture Fragments*, trans. Geoffrey William Bromiley (Grand Rapids, MI: William B. Eerdmans, 1981), sec. 78, 226–27.

and ideological agendas being pushed by these elites and their (oftentimes oblivious) cheerleaders. While real lives hang in the balance, a politics of the spectacle continues to ignore and even exploit the tide of discontentment collecting on the shores of our sense of shared life.

One thing that is clear from this current style of political discourse is that it has increasingly fostered *polarization* and *impasse*, two words that perhaps characterize our current political debates better than anything else. What some commentators have described as a conflict of entrenched ideologies, or culture wars,[7] however, appears to be a less than perspicacious explanation of the real struggle that is actually going on, for below the conflict over morality, family, and education that so energizes and grips proponents of both conservative and liberal ideologies, a more comprehensive sea change is occurring. This shift is a reconfiguration of the state itself, one that is no doubt giving rise to the anxieties that provoke the conflicting ideologies, but one that neither of these ideologies has yet acknowledged. A more profound and disturbing change is taking place, one that clichés and stock phrases cannot resolve no matter how catchy or clever.

The situation we face is much more complicated than our public figures want to acknowledge. Indeed, we are currently experiencing a transformation of our political institutions and the shape of government, a transformation most of us sense but are trained to pay little or no attention to. Out of the nation-state that dominated the past century, a new form of the state is emerging: the market-state. As scholars as diverse as Philip Bobbitt and Bob Jessop have argued, the nation-state is facing a crisis of legitimacy.[8] While the nation-state form originally emerged as a way to

---

7. See James Davidson Hunter, *Culture Wars: The Struggle to Control The Family, Art, Education, Law, and Politics in America* (New York, NY: Basic Books, 1991).

8. Bobbitt, *Shield of Achilles: War, Peace, and the Course of History* (New York, NY: Knopf, 2002), 17. Bobbitt argues that due to innovations that brought an end to the long war, "The nation-state is dying, but this only means that, as in the past, a new form is being born. This new form, the *market-state*, will ultimately be defined by its response to the strategic threats that have made the nation-state no longer viable." He later defines the market-state as "the emerging constitutional order that promises to maximize the opportunity of its people, tending to privatize many state activities and making representative government more responsive to the market" (912). Although we have chosen to use Bobbitt's term *market-state*, Jessop provides a more sophisticated description of this transition by describing the emerging form of the state as a "Schumpeterian workfare post-national regime" (SWPR). See Jessop, *The Future of the Capitalist State* (Cambridge, UK: Polity, 2002), 247. As Jessop argues there, this new form of the state is "replacing the Keynesian welfare national state" (KWNS). This new form is Schumpeterian to the extent that it attempts to promote innovation and flexibility in an overall open economy by intervening on the supply side to increase and strengthen competitiveness in given economic spaces (250). It is workfare in the sense that it submits social policy to the needs and desires of economic policy. Hence, while the "KWNS tried to extend the social rights of its citizens, the SWPR is more concerned to provide welfare services that benefit business and thereby demotes individual needs to second place" (251). Next, it is postnational in that it makes recourse to multilevel and multigovernance institutions such as the International Monetary Fund (IMF), World Bank, European Union (EU), and World Trade Organization (WTO). And finally, it is regime-like to the degree that it relies on the "increased importance of non-state mechanisms in compensating for market failures and inadequacies in the delivery of

provide citizens with a military strong enough to ensure their security, a means of establishing compromise and agreement among a vast constituency, an organized juridical form and tradition, and a method of managing the economic growth of the society so as to guarantee the improvement of everyone's standard of living, it can no longer succeed in fulfilling these functions. As Bobbitt states,

> These tasks were the nation-state's raison d'être. Yet today, market regulation by the State has become unpopular, many citizens have been effectively marginalized in the political life of their societies, and private business organizations have taken the initiative regarding international development. It is they who determine whether the economic policies of a state merit confidence and credit, without which no state can develop. At the same time, there are new security demands on the State that require ever greater executive authority, secrecy, and revenue.[9]

That is to say, the nation-state can no longer ensure for its citizens the rights and goods it was created to provide. In failing to provide its citizens the certainty of security and protection, to restrict international intrusion, to control its own economy, to regulate the proliferation of images and ideas, and to shield its people from ecological hazards or the threat of epidemics, the nation-state cannot perform the tasks that give it its form, resulting in its own disintegration.[10] What is essential to see here is that the nation-state is no longer the functional form of the state and, to the extent that our policy makers, citizens, and government officials act as if it were, it cannot respond adequately to the broader social demands being made upon it. Indeed, it is being eclipsed by a new constitutional arrangement, one wherein the economy plays a much larger role.

For both sides of the partisan political spectrum, this change in the state's makeup is creating deep problems. On the left, liberal Democrats are trapped within the contradiction of inhabiting the economic and geopolitical realities of the market-state while trying to legislate from the nation-state mentality by attempting to implement welfare-state policies. This is shown by the Democrats' persistent belief that an all-out, free market capitalism can still include strong state resources to provide essential social safety nets. The reality is, however, that the very constitution of the market-state conflicts with the provisions of these safety nets, and as a result, it will increasingly collide with them, a clash that can be only temporarily resolved by increasing debt exponentially or making promises that are impossible to fulfill. The contradictions of this perspective were vividly played out in the Democrats' failed attempt to overhaul health care even at a time when they held a supermajority. Democrats are

---

state-sponsored economic and social policies," resulting in a "hollowing out of national states" (254).

9. Bobbitt, *Shield of Achilles*, 208.
10. Ibid., 228.

stuck perpetuating the inefficiencies and failures intrinsic to an increasingly bloated bureaucracy, hopelessly convinced that the nation-state form of government will be able to quell the fracturing effects of a more and more privatized and individualized citizenry under the influence of the market. Thus, their plans are indelibly infused with impotence and failure due to the fact that they both encourage the unfettered economics of the market-state while, at the same time, attempting to offer some consolation to the market's biggest and most persistent losers.

If this were the worst of the current ideologies and programs, things would be bad enough, for we'd be left circling our tails in a never-ending liberal pursuit of complete economic freedom and social responsibility. Yet such a stance has become increasingly innocuous against the Right's move toward a total distrust of the state's role in civic life. If liberal Democrats, confused as they are, are at least dragging their feet into the halls of anarcho-capitalism, then the Right seems set on staying the course in a full-out sprint into this brave new world. For them, an uninhibited free market, American exceptionalism, individualism, shallow civil religion, and a thin, predominantly negative view of freedom have coalesced into a blind faith that private ownership and capital innovation will itself, miraculously, solve the problems. To maintain their devotion to this perspective, the Right's recourse to cliché provides the motivation and energy that keep it moving forward and imbue it with an enduring, if ersatz, legitimacy.

The most recent economic crisis only makes these trends glaringly obvious. This crisis is one that is beyond the government's ability to solve, and any tactic it might take will only distort or tilt the crisis in one direction because the current form of the state, as we have shown, has been completely restructured by the global market. Hence, government programs can no longer make the necessary adjustments to re-establish stability when an economic bubble bursts or when other nations refuse to purchase our debt, making it increasingly difficult for us to raise the debt ceiling. If, as the Marxist thinker David Harvey states, "crises . . . are the irrational rationalizers of an irrational system" and if "there may be no effective long-term capitalist solutions (apart from reversion to fictitious capital manipulations) to this crisis of capitalism" because "at some point quantitative changes lead to qualitative shifts," then we may very well be reaching the moment when there are only irrational, and at best temporary, state solutions to the very real problems we face.[11] Refusing to pursue strategies or resolutions that give the faintest hint of "putting free enterprise on trial,"[12] the political leaders of the Right continue to lead us directly back into the very problems

11. Harvey, *The Enigma of Capital: And the Crisis of Capitalism* (London, UK: Profile Books, 2010), 215–17.

12. Many readers will remember the retort Mitt Romney recently offered to those other candidates who jumped upon his comments regarding the fact that he liked being able to fire people who were providing him with services. In response, he challenged that they were committing this unpardonable sin: putting free enterprise on trial.

and mechanisms that generated the social devastation of this depression. Thus, instead of taking a serious look at the crisis and engaging in real discussion about the problems we face, our political and economic elites return to the same talking points and slogans which give the gloss of solutions even as they solidify our belief that any manipulations of the market, or any state programs, will be felt as an undesired intrusion. It's ultimately a fail-safe tactic because through cliché and slogan they can tout the ability of the free market to resolve any problems, glossing over the fact that a completely free market is already an irrational and impossible ideal, and then point to some interference or government program that disrupted the productive flow of the market when the market inevitably fails.[13]

In this regard, perhaps no other group has employed cliché to a greater effect than the Tea Party. However, rather than dismissing the Tea Party movement as merely a misguided populist performance of right-wing ideology, we believe that underneath all of the banal nostalgia and ideological banter there is a real backlash against the alienating social realities that have accompanied the recent change in the state's makeup. Its charlatan media personalities and billionaire advocates notwithstanding,[14] the average Tea Partier's intuition of the emerging market-state stems from a perceived loss of authentic American cultural unity—that is, the white, Protestant, and middle-class identity perfected during the postwar "golden years" of late industrial capitalism.[15] Feeling the social degradation of a consumer subjectivity that has reduced the idea of a shared public life down to a shallow and culturally indifferent economic pragmatism, the Tea Party is more aware than many would like

13. Karl Polanyi, *The Great Transformation: The Political and Economic Origins of Our Time* (1944; Boston, MA: Beacon, 2001), 3. In this volume, Polanyi directly challenges the ideological and historical utopianism implicit in the notion of a self-regulating, free market. Indeed, he shows the degree to which this utopianism so strained the social life of Europe that it helped to create the conditions that precipitated the rise of fascism, leading to World War II. A self-regulating and totally free market, he argues, is a fiction, for it has never existed and never will.

14. With media figures such as Glenn Beck and Sean Hannity and financial moguls like the Koch brothers, a new form of celebrity has emerged from the reverb of those feeling alienated by this regime. Yet, both as a testament to the idolatrous nature of this empire and to its ingenious ability to sell back to us our own frustration with it, this new celebrity capitalizes on the degrading effects of neoliberal policies not by pointing to its flaws and devastating effects on society, but instead by dusting off this ideology and asserting that these failures have resulted from our infidelity to the self-regulating free market.

15. The identity politics of the Tea Party's predominantly white and Protestant makeup should be framed in what Étienne Balibar calls "fictive ethnicity," the imaginary and constructed ethnic base that legitimates the idea of a nation's historic and "natural" preexisting unity. Balibar writes, "No nation possesses an ethnic base naturally, but as social formations are nationalized, the populations included within them, divided up among them or dominated by them are ethnicized—that is, represented in the past or in the future *as if* they formed a natural community, possessing of itself an identity of origins, culture and interests which transcends individuals and social conditions" (Balibar, "The Nation Form: History and Ideology," in *Race, Nation, Class: Ambiguous Identities*, by Balibar and Immanuel Wallerstein [New York, NY: Verso, 1991], 96). The racism inherent in the rhetoric and policy proposals of the Tea Party might best be understood from within Balibar's theories of the nation form and fictive ethnicity.

to admit of the social injustices and alienation of the emerging market-state. And the Tea Party is even more attuned to the government's inability to provide the essential social goods of life when it makes recourse to the social welfare programs of the nation-state. The Tea Party knows that the average American has been disenfranchised by a state that has become the handmaiden of Wall Street rather than the insurer of public goods; it knows that an unregulated free market has meant that the state has little ability to do anything about Joe-factory-worker's 401(k) being gambled away by stockbrokers and hedge-fund managers; it knows that the commodification of all social relationships by market forces has meant the collapse of any sense of a shared public good. Even if its members are unable to articulate these realities, they certainly feel them and intuit correctly that the government can no longer perform the tasks of the nation-state.

Yet herein lies the great contradiction of the Tea Party and its inability to penetrate the complexities of the current situation: while it vociferously defends the market-state's most general and clichéd aspects as the essential conditions of freedom—unregulated market, small government, a meritocratic competitive workfare, et cetera—it articulates the need to restore favorable social and economic conditions to its constituency by running further into the very alienation that the free market has created in the first place. Instead of recognizing the emerging market-state and its drive toward total social alienation, cliché provides the Tea Party with the means to avoid having to admit the massive contradictions inherent in its politics. Rather than assessing the deeper structural realities that are fueling the emergence of the market-state, the Tea Party has instead conjured a substitutionary image on which to unleash their frustration: liberal Democrats' paternalistic and atavistic insistence that the government should be telling citizens how to think about the common good through programs of social welfare. In this way, the absolute vilification and dismissal of liberal Democrats and all forms of big government is rooted not necessarily in ideological opposition (although this is certainly a major part of it) but in dissatisfaction with the failure and inability of the social programs of the welfare-state to create and mediate a common good. In their perception of Democrats—and not the inherent, and therefore more difficult to perceive, aspects of the emerging market-state—as attempting to stifle the transcendental providence of the market's ability to provide utopian conditions for personal liberty, the Tea Party's emphasis on the clichés of freedom, liberty, and bourgeois morality can be viewed as a sort of rhetorical defense mechanism against the dehumanizing effect of both the market-state's actual indifference toward cultural unity (unrecognized but felt) and the political paternalism of the Democratic party (recognized and exploited). In this way, the Tea Party can avoid the hard and honest work of assessing the more savage side of free market capitalism's transformation of the state, casting all cares upon the market.

As we have already hinted, the Tea Party speaks to an underlying truth of our contemporary political situation. By saying this, we mean to recognize that the Tea Party language of "less government" only makes sense within what Alasdair MacIntyre has called a "predominantly Weberian" society, wherein collective life is organized around and through a central bureaucratic apparatus.[16] In order to flesh this out, we will examine why these people feel, as many of us do, that a government "for, of, by the people" has come to be felt as an external intrusion on our lives. We need to recognize why bureaucratic management has replaced a unified sense of the good.

We can only begin to understand this if we consider the way in which our modern societies are dominated by economic relations, the way in which our political economy has largely replaced politics in our lives. To the extent that individuality reigns within modern societies like that of America—that is to say, to the extent that the basis of a political economy is grounded in each individual's pursuit of her own self-interest—the unifying principle of that society can no longer be some sense of a common good. Instead, where the emphasis on self-interest displaces an emphasis on the common good, this society will require the construction of a bureaucracy to structure the fabric of common life in order to assuage the forces of dissolution. And this bureaucracy will need to grow in direct proportion to the increasing sense of alienation created by the diffusive momentum of self-interest. Thus, people within this society will come to experience their interaction with this mediating bureaucracy as more and more an experience of external coercion, outside interference, and annoyance. They will come to see it as an intrusion upon their own sense of the good, leading them to resent it and to seek to limit it further. Yet this interest in reducing the bureaucracy of government is based in a deep contradiction, for to limit or restrict governmental intervention is to threaten the very fabric of social life. That is, to attack the bureaucracy is to attack what remains of the unifying threads of our communal life within a political economy. Hence, although the bureaucracy is perceived to be the ever-encroaching arm of external rule, it is at the same time the very internal fabric of our life together and, as it wears thin, more and more folks are left to brave the turbulent seas of the unfettered market alone, further alienating them from one another.

Therefore, what the Tea Party advocates make evident, even in their willingness to live with this contradiction, is the degree to which the social ligaments of our lives have been stretched to the breaking point, stretched to the point that in the name of

---

16. MacIntyre, *After Virtue: A Study in Moral Theory*, 2nd ed. (Notre Dame, IN: University of Notre Dame Press, 1984), 109. Readers who are familiar with this important text will recognize that MacIntyre makes this statement at the beginning of the central chapter in the book. Sans a collective view of the common good and a positive vision of freedom, MacIntyre asserts that there are only two possible ways forward for a society trapped within the "iron cage" of management and bureaucracy which has filled the void left by the absence of these unifying goods: Nietzsche and Aristotle.

patriotism people want to go at it on their own. This is the truth we must learn from the Tea Party: the bureaucratic nature of our communal life is reaching its limit; to the extent that economics has come to dominate our social relations, we no longer possess an ability to produce a coherent vision of the shared, good life, and so an American political bureaucracy of the common good strikes us as paternalism and intrusion, leaving us profoundly alienated.

Returning to Arendt's depiction of cliché and evil in relation to Eichmann, we cannot help but think that the current poverty of real political discourse is symptomatic of an underlying depreciation of our communal life and that this depreciation is connected in a very real way to capitalism. As our lives have become increasingly commodified, like every other commodity under capitalism, they have grown cheaper and cheaper and we experience this diminishment of our lives in our language and discourse. And thus we can begin to see how a capitalism that has escaped its container truly starts to enact an evil upon our social lives.[17] Because it is essentially a deprivation of reality, as the theologian Herbert McCabe reminds us, "evil has meaning only at a fairly superficial level," and hence, the banal and clichéd talk that accompanies this unchallenged embrace of capital cooperates with it and "diminishes life." Trusting the superficiality of our clichés and refusing to engage in robust arguments about how to move forward, the paucity of our dialogue further advances the depreciation of our lives. This impoverishment is most manifest in our inability to truly listen to other voices, to entertain and discuss any alternative that questions the good of market growth or profit. The superficiality of sloganizing and pat answers belies the underlying fear that is intrinsic to evil: the fear of making oneself vulnerable to others, of really being able to question one's way of life. Acting in this fear, then, the tendency, particularly in American political debates, is to aim for domination instead of communication, in part because communication "disturbs our present world, lays it open to influence from others, which may involve revolutionary change."[18] Real communication around the current economic crisis and real political discourse that could lead us off this banal road to perdition and into a deeper level of human meaning would, we think, involve allowing us to hear from a sustained and deep critique of capitalism.

17. Commenting on the point at which capitalism comes to act as an oppressive power over our lives, political scientist Wendy Brown notes, "When capital radically escapes both its container and its limits in the nation-state, when it becomes a genuinely global power, it acquires many of the specifically religious trappings of sovereignty—absolute, enduring, supreme, decisive about life and death, beyond human control, and above all beyond accountability to law or morality" ("The Sacred, the Secular, and the Profane: Charles Taylor and Karl Marx," in *Varieties of Secularism in a Secular Age*, ed. Michael Warner, Jonathan Van Antwerpen, and Craig Calhoun [Cambridge, MA: Harvard University Press, 2010], 103). Interestingly enough, Brown goes on to discuss the seemingly non-exteriority to capital in our day, lamenting the totalizing breadth of its reach and ultimately pointing to the necessity of fringe movements that oppose the all-encompassing reign of capital (104).

18. McCabe, *Law, Love and Language* (1968; New York, NY: Continuum, 2003), 100–101.

In a fractured world where it often seems impossible to know how to connect all the elements and pieces of our lives, where the tasks of our individual professions seem detached from any larger story of what is going on, the temptation is always to rely on simple clichés and slogans that appear to bring it all together in simple solutions. As the theologians David Burrell and Stanley Hauerwas have noted, this is because "our endemic need for order—the demand we experience to make a story of our lives—also presses us to forge a unity before we have discovered one adequate to our situation." As a result, we are constantly prone to self-deception[19] and to living demonic, because untruthful, forms of life. To this extent, we believe that a church working to understand itself within the narrative of Christ has even more reason to listen to a thorough critique of capital. Because it is in Christ and in the believing community that we know what is going on in the world, we ought to have the freedom to step back and interrogate the power the market has gained over our lives. We ought to have the freedom to name the deception inherent in all stock phrases about "common sense," "Give me liberty not debt," "Obamacare," "It's the spending stupid!" or even "winning the future." Based on such discernment, we will see that these slogans signify a world that has no future because it has been frozen within the order and ideology of a capitalism that promotes itself as an unmovable and eternal truth.

Contrary to the illusion of such slogans, Christ's life cannot be contained within the order of capitalism; his life disrupts all claims of mastery and opens up the future to new and unforeseen possibilities of living in the world. Christ's life, however, does not provide merely another slogan, as if it only represents another cliché of political engagement. Rather, Christ's life is that mode of being human in which the world is always received as a gift, the mode of being human which is utterly free because it abides in obedience to God and therefore cannot be handled or mastered through predetermined categories of human action. And to resist the order of futureless consumption and unlimited production and accumulation and to work toward a genuine future of shared good, we must participate in Christ's life. Only if we are ready and willing to give ourselves over to this life might we find a way forward that is more creative than the market and more unifying than the addition of yet another organ to the bureaucracy.

In conclusion, if we are right about the fact that a poverty of discourse and language is one indication of a movement toward the demonic, as was certainly the case with Eichmann, then we think that we as Christians ought to pursue a complexification and deepening of the political discourse, not its naive simplification. If left to the current trajectory, the likelihood of our traveling a similar road to that of Eichmann's is an all-too-real possibility. No doubt, hints of such a path are already

---

19. Burrell and Hauerwas, "Self-Deception and Autobiography: Reflections on Speer's *Inside the Third Reich* (1974)," in *The Hauerwas Reader*, ed. John Berkman and Michael Cartwright (Durham, NC: Duke University Press, 2001), 217.

evident in the banal and vapid soundings of empty and ideological sloganeering that can easily channel anger and frustration into violence. The simplistic rhetoric of deportation that accompanies anti-immigration vitriol, the clichéd reduction of the problem of unemployment and worker welfare to superficial beliefs in flexibility and market provision, and the illusion of certainty provided by war-cry slogans that stamp out the real casualties and costs of war—these examples may indicate that the conditions of superficiality that characterize the banal road to perdition may already be in place. Disrupting the slogans and clichés with a more attentive and detailed discourse, taking the time to consider the complexities and complications of living in our world, may be critical to resisting evil's diminishment of our lives. After all, if Christ has given us lives that are worth living, then the structures and goods of this life are probably worthy of the attention that a thoughtful and rigorous argument would encourage.

5 The Killer in Me Is the Killer in You: An Interview with Richard Beck

by CHRIS KELLER

In his book *Unclean*, Richard Beck offers a unique, incisive look at the psychological dynamics at work within the church. Through the prisms of experimental and social psychology, he exposes key psychological barriers that prevent us from fully participating in the life of the church, particularly in church missiology. In this interview, Beck shares insight from *Unclean* and discusses the ways in which these barriers may signal the end of empathy and the beginning of evil.

The Other Journal (TOJ): P. J. Watson recently argued that Christianity and psychology operate from "essentially different systems of rationality."[1] Your book *Unclean* is a remarkable piece of integrative work between experimental psychology and theology that is mindful to possible interdisciplinary problems yet relatively unencumbered in navigating between disciplines. Do you share Watson's sentiment, and if so, how do you navigate these potentially competing rationalities in your work as a Christian experimental psychologist?

Richard Beck (RB): That's an interesting question because it highlights the different texture of my work in comparison to a lot of what you find in the literature integrating psychology and Christianity. Historically, and still today, most of the work in the integration of psychology and Christianity has focused on psychotherapy and has been done by clinical and counseling psychologists. This focus on the therapeutic moment has created a host of interesting problems. Embedded in psychological

---

1. See Watson, "Whose Psychology? Which Rationality? Christian Psychology within an Ideological Surround after Postmodernism," *Journal of Psychology and Christianity* 4 (2011): 307; and Beck, *Unclean: Meditations on Purity, Hospitality, and Mortality* (Eugene, OR: Cascade Books, 2011).

theories of behavior change and human flourishing are a number of Enlightenment and humanistic assumptions, and many of these assumptions don't sit well with certain Christian anthropologies and epistemologies, particularly those from Reformed or Calvinistic traditions.

Here is where I'm a bit different: I'm an experimental psychologist whose research focuses less on clinical or counseling psychology than on topics from social and personality psychology, the "psychology of everyday life" as I describe it to my students. Thus, I've published on such topics as humor, gossip, profanity, death anxiety, beliefs about Satan, attitudes about the incarnation—for example, did Jesus experience nocturnal emissions or diarrhea? Opinions differ—and why Christian bookstore art is so bad, or what I call the Thomas Kinkade Effect. In my research I'm not thinking about the therapy room but about the everyday experience of Christians in the world. There's not a lot of research on subjects like this, so it feels different and fresh. Moreover, it rarely gets tangled up in issues related to epistemology and anthropology. For the curious, a lot of my research is summarized in *Unclean* and in my just-released book, *The Authenticity of Faith*.

TOJ: The biblical text that inspired *Unclean* is in Matthew 9 and Matthew 12, where Jesus tells the Pharisees, "I require mercy, not sacrifice" (NIV). Could you briefly sketch for us how you understand these two constructs?

RB: In *Unclean*, I'm building on the work of Walter Brueggemann and Fernando Belo. As they argue it, within the life of Israel there were two competing visions of uprightness before God—the Levitical or priestly vision and the prophetic or justice vision. The Levitical tradition focused on the experience of cultic purity before God whereas the prophetic tradition focused on rehabilitative activity to care for the poor and marginalized. However, as Brueggemann notes, these impulses live in "profound tension" with each other. They are, in fact, often at an impasse. So when we reach Jesus in Matthew 9, we see him stepping into a conflict that isn't fully resolved in the Old Testament. Which tradition should be privileged in the life of Israel? What does God demand? To use the words of Miroslav Volf, should the church function through "exclusion or embrace"?[2] Thus, when we see Jesus quote Hosea in Matthew 9:13—"I desire mercy, not sacrifice"—we can read this as Jesus decisively privileging the prophetic tradition in the life of Israel. Eating with "tax collectors and sinners" (Matt. 9:11) is the proper understanding of what it means to be upright before God

---

2. For more on the two competing visions of uprightness see Brueggemann, *Theology of the Old Testament: Testimony, Dispute, Advocacy* (Minneapolis, MN: Fortress, 1997), 192–95; and Belo, *A Materialist Reading of the Gospel of Mark* (Maryknoll, NY: Orbis Books, 1981). Also, see Volf, *Exclusion and Embrace: A Theological Exploration of Identity, Otherness, and Reconciliation* (Nashville, TN: Abingdon, 1996).

as opposed to standing with the Pharisees who were excluding such people in the pursuit of Levitical purity.

Here's how all this plays out psychologically: My sense is that a lot of churches think they can have it both ways. You often see this in the common refrain "love the sinner but hate the sin." The psychological research I review in *Unclean* suggests that this maxim is almost impossible to put into practice. Psychologically speaking, mercy and purity pull us in opposite directions. And behaviorally, as we see in Matthew 9, we have to make a choice: follow Jesus as he crosses the purity boundary or stand with the Pharisees who have opted for quarantine.

TOJ: Scapegoating, the communal expulsion or punishing of an individual for the cohesion of the overall community, is important in your book. With the presidential elections ramping up and the perpetuation of a depressed economy still bearing down on many in this country, how do you see both the tendency to scapegoat and *infrahumanize* in popular discourse?

RB: *Infrahumanization* is a psychological term that refers to seeing out-group members as less than fully human. It is the psychological process that drives the experience and discourse of Otherness. This is usually accomplished by denying the out-group member some key characteristic that is possessed by the in-group. Generally, the Other is seen as less intelligent or morally inferior—Others are dishonest, depraved, lazy, or lacking in self-discipline. In extreme cases, Others are seen as hostile and malevolent agents intent on doing members of the in-group harm. This is the nadir of infrahumanization, the creation of the monster.

Moving to the current political discourse this election year, I was struck by something Newt Gingrich said at the Republican primary debate in South Carolina. In talking about how to deal with terrorists, Gingrich said that Americans should adopt Andrew Jackson's method of dealing with our enemies: kill them. Just-war theology aside, the category of *enemy* can be pretty slippery. Who gets to define *enemy*? Moreover, enemies are infrahumans. Thus, once the enemy card is played, our moral responsibilities and the care we take in moral self-criticism are attenuated. All of this should be worrisome to Christians, who are taught that our enemies are not "flesh and blood" (Eph. 6:12).

Beyond the War on Terror, I worry about the discourse of Otherness as it's currently playing out in regard to legal and illegal immigrants, Iran, socioeconomic class, same-sex marriage, and the unemployed. But really, our entire political discourse has been reduced to a discourse of Otherness. There isn't an issue today that doesn't involve the American public choosing sides and dehumanizing those who disagree.

TOJ: As I read *Unclean*, I found myself thinking about how experiences of trauma ossify communities against hospitality, about how disgust and purity psychologies realize purity through expulsion of the impure. How do these psychological factors interface, and do you think Christian communities need to understand trauma more robustly to be missional communities?

RB: At root, disgust is a protective mechanism. Disgust monitors the orifices of the body, mainly oral incorporation, to protect and preserve the integrity of the body. If we've been traumatized—personally or communally—we will seek to establish boundaries and we will become hypervigilant in monitoring those boundaries. Sometimes boundaries are forcibly violated and sometimes we embrace others (allowing them inside our bodies or communities) only to have our trust violated. These are wounds that can go beyond all words, leaving deep scars in our hearts and memories. Consequently, it is only natural that individuals and communities will move forward cautiously, even suspiciously. To protect ourselves we turn inward rather than outward.

In *Unclean* I don't question the establishment of boundaries in these sorts of cases. These times of inwardness and self-protection are important. The main thing I try to point out in *Unclean* is simply that we should recognize what is going on in all this. If a church community has been burned in some way, there will be a season of healing inwardness. This is a therapeutic choice. But a therapeutic community will struggle to be a missional community.

I think this might be one reason that some post-Christian and emergent churches struggle to become missional. Many of the people who are attracted to these communities have been deeply hurt by churches. Thus, they seek communities of therapy and healing. But when should that season end? When should the church stop serving as a spiritual hospital, a place where my emotional needs are met, and instead become a place where I'm equipped for mission? I think a lot of churches are trying to figure this out, and they are getting a lot of push back when they try to make the transition. It's difficult to be therapeutic and prophetic at the same time.

TOJ: In *Unclean* you analyze the metaphors that are used in Scripture to illuminate sin and redemption,[3] and then you propose that we may rely too heavily on such metaphors. Could you talk about how Christians might overuse metaphor and about how Christians might keep themselves open and perceptive to theological nuance?

---

3. See Beck, *Unclean*, 35, which lists nineteen of these metaphors for sin and evil.

RB: I'm building on the work of George Lakoff who has done extensive work on how metaphors help us ground and reason through abstractions.[4] For example, we often reason about good versus bad through an orientational up-versus-down metaphor. Good is up (e.g., "You've lifted my spirits"), and bad is down (e.g., "Don't sink to their level"). As I discussed in *Unclean*, cleanliness appears to be an innate and intuitive metaphor for understanding good versus bad, with clean indicative of good and unclean indicative of bad. This metaphor fills the Old and New Testaments and saturates the Christian experience. Sin is defilement, uncleanliness, and contamination; grace is being made clean and pure, "washed as white as snow" (Ps. 51:7).

The issue here isn't about the poetry. As Lakoff shows, we use these metaphors as cognitive aids. The metaphors give us a logic that can help us reason through airy abstractions. For example, if a relationship is *broken*, the logic is that it can be *fixed*. In some ways this metaphorical logic is helpful. It promotes hope. But the metaphor can be just as unhelpful. Can a relationship get fixed like, say, we fix a broken car? The broken/fixed metaphor, while hopeful, isn't equipped to capture the full drama of relational reconciliation. Consequently, we prefer metaphors like *healing* rather than fixing when we talk about relationships. *Healing* better captures the slow and difficult process of reconciliation. It also lets us know that setbacks are anticipated and natural.

The point for our purposes is that the clean/unclean and pure/impure metaphors—which are so ubiquitous within Christianity—while natural and helpful, can be problematic as well. For example, once we are "clean," we have to beware of what Chen-Bo Zhong and Katie Liljenquist have dubbed the Macbeth Effect, where the experience of being clean can come to replace moral effort.[5] This is the psychology underneath a classic spiritual formation problem: the privileging of justification over sanctification. Once made clean, there seems little left to do, spiritually speaking, for the new Christian. It doesn't make much sense, metaphorically speaking, to be *more* clean.

Thus, if used unreflectively or too frequently, purity metaphors can activate psychological processes that de-energize and demotivate faith communities. We need to pay attention to the metaphors we're using and the associated psychology we're activating. When people already feel clean, any change, particularly changes involving an engagement with outsiders, is seen as too risky. All you'll do, following the logic of the metaphor, is make a mess of things. It's safer to maintain purity with acts of quarantine. Just think about how you feel when you buy a new white shirt or dress—that cautiousness, that desire to protect the shirt, is the same cautiousness we

---

4. See, for example, Lakoff and Mark Johnson, *Metaphors We Live By* (Chicago, IL: University of Chicago Press, 1980).

5. Zhong and Liljenquist, "Washing Away Your Sins: Threatened Morality and Physical Cleansing," *Science* 313 (2006): 1451–52.

import into the life of the church through purity metaphors. Missional communities just can't be that jittery.

TOJ: One of my favorite parts of *Unclean* is your discussion of the typical psychological makeups of conservatives and liberals, as well as the ways in which the dialogue between these different psychological modes leads to dumbfounding. I found myself thinking about where positive psychology or virtue psychology might participate in this conversation—what types of character strengths or virtues do you view as important for Christians to cultivate in order to remain in dialogue with people of different psychological constitutions? Can the cultivation of virtues lead to less dumbfounding and a more faithful witness, and how might it specifically be effective vis-à-vis the different ways people are offended?

RB: Here I'm using the work of Jonathan Haidt regarding the ways in which conservatives and liberals differ in how they use various *moral grammars* to make judgments of right versus wrong.[6] Liberals tend to restrict their moral judgments to issues related to harm and justice. Conservatives, by contrast, also appeal to moral criteria related to purity and sanctity. The classic example is how conservatives and liberals view the issue of same-sex marriage. Where liberals will see the issue as one of basic fairness and equality, conservatives, while not immune to those arguments, will tend to privilege a concern for the sanctity of marriage. Here the moral grammar of purity and sanctity trumps the criteria of justice and harm.

Beyond this basic disagreement between liberals and conservatives regarding which moral criterion should trump another in any given situation, I go on in *Unclean* to discuss Haidt's work on moral dumbfounding. Simply put, no one agrees on what exactly constitutes a purity or sanctity violation. Here's a simple example: What is the proper attire for a worship service? Opinions differ, and there is no publicly available criteria that can be marshaled to bring about consensus. People just have different sensibilities about this and so conflict is inevitable.

Here's the connection with positive and virtue psychology: The moral dumbfounding research suggests that moral judgments are largely affective and unconscious. This research sides with the moral tradition of David Hume over Immanuel Kant; as Hume says, "Reason . . . is the slave of the passions."[7] Our moral judgments tend to be quick and instinctive rather than well reasoned and reflective. Moreover, our reasoned explanations are often found to be ad hoc rationalizations for what we feel to be true in our guts.

---

6. See Haidt, *The Righteous Mind: Why Good People Are Divided by Politics and Religion* (New York, NY: Pantheon, 2012).

7. Hume and L. A. Selby-Bigge, *A Treatise of Human Nature* (Oxford, UK: Clarendon, 1896), 685.

The implication here for churches is that most churches privilege cognition over emotion in their spiritual formation efforts. Educational models dominate. We focus on teaching, catechesis, and doctrine. In contrast, advances in positive and virtue psychology, which have paralleled similar trends in the spiritual formation literature, are focusing less on cognition than upon virtue formation in envisioning the moral agent. What is needed in our churches is not more education but more embodied practices that can shape our affections and behavior along with our attitudes. The virtues I focus on in *Unclean* involve the practices of welcome and hospitality, what Volf calls "the will to embrace."[8]

TOJ: What specific virtues do you find necessary in cultivating Volf's "will to embrace"? And what particular embodied practices do you see contributing to the nurturing of these virtues?

RB: I would argue that the will to embrace primarily involves the virtues of perspective taking, empathy, and kindness. In *Unclean*, I talk about Peter Singer's notion of the moral circle. Inside the moral circle my "kin" are treated with "kindness" and those on the outside are treated as "strangers." So I'd argue that the will to embrace is, following Singer, an expansion of the moral circle to include others, extending familial warmth and affection to those not formally of my "tribe."[9] It is to live in the world as if there were no strangers. And the key virtues in making this happen are cognitive (perspective taking), affective (empathy), and behavioral (kindness).

As far as embodied practices go, I'd argue for the practice of friendship. One problem with a lot of outreach ministries and mission efforts is that the interactions between the church and, say, the poor are hierarchical. These ministries are service- or outcome-oriented rather than relational. We come in, do some goods deeds, and then exit the scene until our next mission trip or outreach effort. Although these activities are generally good things in and of themselves, I don't think these sorts of hierarchical interactions create the virtues of hospitality. Friendships, given their mutuality and egalitarian nature, are better positioned to do this. So that's where I would start. If you want to practice the virtues associated with the will to embrace, start expanding your friendship circle to include those people who look a bit different than yourself. Eat, as Jesus did, with the tax collectors and sinners of the world.

---

8. Volf, *Exclusion and Embrace*, 216.

9. See Singer, *The Expanding Circle: Ethics, Evolution, and Moral Progress* (Princeton, NJ: Princeton University Press, 2011).

TOJ: This issue of *The Other Journal* is on evil. Given the trajectory of *Unclean*, how does disgust psychology shape your hamartiology and inform your understanding of evil?

RB: One could argue that our discussion here might be the most important discussion in the entire issue. Evil doesn't come out of nowhere, and the people who commit atrocities (or even small acts of exclusion and meanness) don't describe themselves as evil; most of the evil done in the world is done by people who think they are doing the right thing. And until we understand that dynamic, we aren't going to be very effective in combating the darkness in the world. More than anything else, evil is a psychological problem. Most perpetrators feel like they are the real victims and that their actions are very much justified. And to commit the worst atrocities (e.g., genocide, rape, torture, slavery), you need the psychology of infrahumanization—you need to see the Other as less than fully human.

Socio-moral disgust, the psychology I discuss in *Unclean*, sits at the center of all this. As Martha Nussbaum has observed, "Throughout history, certain disgust properties—sliminess, bad smell, stickiness, decay, foulness—have repeatedly and monotonously been associated with, indeed projected onto, groups by reference to whom privileged groups seek to define their superior human status."[10] Once that psychology is in play nothing stands between us and the demonic.

---

10. Nussbaum, *Upheavals of Thought: The Intelligence of Emotions* (Cambridge, UK: Cambridge University Press, 2003), 347.

6 The Terrible and Sublime Liturgy: A Meditation on Evil, Scapegoats, and Beauty

by AGUSTÍN MAES

"Police arrest teenage mother of dead newborn."
"Ohio cult leader executed for murdering family of four."
"Man found guilty of drowning three-year-old stepdaughter for insurance money."
"Chilling testimony in trial of roofer charged with torture, murder."
"Police, family, hope for tips in teen girl's 'horrific' slaying."
"Witnesses describe brutal beating on country road."

These are news stories clipped from newspapers and pinned on a corkboard that hangs on a wall near my kitchen. I see them every day.[1]

I'm a messy person—a typical guy not too bothered by his own untidiness and general grunge. There are piles of books and papers scattered around my apartment, stacks of unopened junk mail, the collection of San Francisco Giants bobbleheads arranged near my desk covered in a light layer of dust, vases of dried-out flowers never tossed out. I don't entertain guests and so I don't bother to pick up very often. But I did have an overnight guest some months ago. My friend Richard, who lives on Bainbridge Island, slept on my sofa hide-a-bed during the first night of an unusual December cold snap. He noticed the journalistic tales of evil pinned to my corkboard while I made up his bed.

"What's up with these?" he asked.

---

1. This essay is adapted from the Keynote Address at Milton Center Forum, Seattle Pacific University, June 3, 2010.

"Story ideas," I told him sheepishly.

"Grim," Richard said.

Though I knew he thought it was a little strange, Richard's take on my collection of newspaper clippings fits into his understanding of who I am. We've been friends for many years. But anyone else who might come over and see the yellowing newspaper articles—someone who doesn't know me—would certainly wonder about the collage of true-life horrors pinned to my wall as informally as recipes or supermarket coupons. That person might even get uneasy and begin to speculate about my psychological equilibrium. But the thing is, the events reported in the newspaper clippings I collect make *me* uneasy. I find their true stories of evil difficult to comprehend. I also find them irresistible. Part of this is because they titillate me, I admit. But there is something else about the clippings, something that goes beyond titillation.

Whether we admit it or not, haven't we all slowed down to rubberneck while passing automobile accidents or police arrests? It's in our nature to go by a car crash with a certain sense of acquittal; we may feel a bit of *schadenfreude* at the spectacle of a guy getting handcuffed against a patrol car, perhaps while on our way to take in a production of *Sweeney Todd: Demon Butcher of Fleet Street*. Then, back at home, we might watch a little television before going to bed, turning up the volume and craning our heads when we hear "the following images may be disturbing for some viewers." We gawk at the ghastly while brushing our teeth. We cope with darkness by regarding it from a distance, by acknowledging it in polite, sanitized terms: "Isn't that awful? Can you imagine?" What we're really saying, what we won't admit to, is that we think he deserved it, she was a tramp, or that that boy wasn't right in the head.

As I said, I'm a typical guy. I don't mop or vacuum very frequently. I don't do laundry until my socks and underwear are running out. But my kitchen must be clean. An unclean kitchen sets my teeth on edge. Every morning while doing the dishes I see the corkboard. Though the news clippings serve as inspiration for story ideas, they also serve another purpose, something that resists definition. I begin each day doing dishes in the company of murderers, the insane, the terrified, the despised and rejected. I begin the day with reports of appalling acts of violence: "Newborn girl found dead in trash bin." My light breakfast—yogurt and fruit, maybe a little oatmeal—includes reminders of our capacity for evil and of our desire to condemn, maybe in an attempt at making evil go away. We have always done this: "And he shall put them upon the head of the goat, and send him away into the wilderness by the hand of a man who is in readiness. The goat shall bear all their iniquities upon him to a solitary land; and he shall let the goat go into the wilderness" (Lev. 16:21b–22 RSV). We all want people we can hate. We want figures we can saddle with our sins and consign to the windswept barrens, both criminals and the victims of those criminals' terrible acts, both the guilty and innocent. At the supermarket, for example, I can't resist opening up the tabloids, eagerly devouring snippets of stories on Lindsay Lohan or Charlie Sheen or the love child of former vice presidential candidate John Edwards. And then I'll buy my coffee and oranges and split pea soup and walk through the automatic doors to the parking lot, reassured of my oh-so-upstanding self, of my relative cleanliness.

In her essay "The Love of God and Affliction," Simone Weil wrote, "If a hen is hurt, the others rush up and peck it. The phenomenon is as automatic as gravitation. Our senses attach to affliction all the contempt, all the revulsion, all the hatred which our reason attaches to crime. Except for those whose soul is inhabited by Christ, everybody despises the afflicted to some extent, although practically no one is conscious of it."[2]

I grew up with chickens whose eggs I had to collect in the mornings: dirty animals whose coop I had to clean, fending off an attacking rooster every day after school. I know firsthand the phenomenon Weil describes. And I've seen the same phenomenon in the behavior of human beings: in the schoolyard, at work, on the street, in myself. How many of us have souls truly inhabited by Christ?

"Dad gets twenty-five years for microwaving girl."

There are other things pinned to my corkboard besides newspaper clippings: a copper cross given to me by my longtime girlfriend's parents, prayer cards of the Virgin Mary and the Apostle Paul, icons of the Archangel Michael and Nicholas of Myra, and a postcard bought at the Church of the Gesù in Rome three years ago. The postcard is a reproduction of Jacopino del Conte's portrait of Saint Ignatius of Loyola, founder of the Society of Jesus and patron saint of my parish in San Francisco; his expression serene and meditative, he wears a biretta, head circled by a thin golden nimbus.

Media vita in morte sumus. These are the opening words of a medieval Gregorian responsorial, words I wrote down on a strip of paper I keep near a human skull I own, something given to me by my Bainbridge Island friend Richard who had once been my roommate in a small tenement apartment in Manhattan. When he got engaged and returned to his native West, he left me the skull. It now rests on my bookshelf. The skull has a triangular hole cut into its right side near the crown, the vestige of some surgery probably meant for medical students to observe by way of demonstration. I try and show the skull respect, knowing it was once a person—*is* a person—an old person as evidenced by the tightly knit seams joining its frontal, parietal, and occipital plates: a person whose former life is a mystery to me. But this skull is more than a simple *memento mori*, more than the remnant of a person whose life I know nothing of. It is also a reminder of the greater mystery we are all immersed in.

---

2. Weil, *Simone Weil: Writings Selected with an Introduction by Eric O. Springsted*, ed. Eric O. Springsted, Modern Spiritual Masters Series (Maryknoll, NY: Orbis Books, 1998), 45.

The Jesuit paleontologist Pierre Teilhard de Chardin wrote in his book *The Divine Milieu*, "By means of all created things, without exception, the divine assails us, penetrates us, and molds us. We imagined it as distant and inaccessible, whereas in fact we live steeped in its burning layers." The great Jesuit theologian Karl Rahner made a similar observation, writing that humankind is rooted in an infinite horizon of being: the "transcendental existential." This rootedness, our awareness of infinite being that cannot be grasped but is still experienced, is a condition, Rahner wrote, that is the "basic mode of being which is prior to and permeates every objective experience."[3] We all pre-apprehend the infinite—what Rahner termed *Vorgriff*—that which is beyond our comprehension but within which we participate because of our own finitude.

The skull on my bookshelf is illustrative of that finitude, the triangular hole in its right parietal plate a window through which to glimpse much more than the simple fact of mortality. That relic and substance of an unknown person once had lips to whistle with, to hail a cab in New York City, to cheer at a cricket match in Trinidad or while working at a shipyard in Calcutta. I will never know. The skull—a thing I do not really own and can never really own—rests beside a photograph of my mother in the black-and-white habit of the Sisters of Divine Providence, a sister in the order's St. Louis Province for thirteen years before answering to her other vocation: motherhood. She is a person I obviously *did* know.

Media vita in morte sumus—"In the midst of life we are in death." These words were branded on me at a young age.

When I was twenty I stroked my mother's forehead in a room furnished, I suppose, to provide a sense of comfort: softly lit and windowless, a small sofa and chair placed along two of the walls, upholstered in ordinary shades of green and violet; it was a kind of peculiar waiting room. There was also a gurney in the room on which rested what remained of a sudden and severe Christmas Eve cerebral infarction. Her brow was impossibly cold and strangely oily, eyelids not completely shut but three-quarters lidded, teeth jutting fishlike from a weird mockery of a mouth. My father, stricken by the first hours of a grief that would debilitate him for the rest of his life, pulled the sheet up over that mouth-not-a-mouth and stood back, the new features in his expression working their way into his face: a years-long makeover only Lon Chaney could have imitated. He had been a sergeant in the elite First Marine Reconnaissance Battalion, a stoic, self-possessed man who had done a tour on a submarine, who had ridden in landing ships and tanks and bubble helicopters. The First Recon Battalion's motto was, and remains, "Swift, Silent, Deadly." The sight of his shock intensified my own fright.

---

3. Chardin, *The Divine Milieu: An Essay on the Interior Life*, trans. William Collins (New York, NY: Harper & Row, 1960), 112; and Rahner, *Foundations of Christian Faith: An Introduction to the Idea of Christianity*, trans. William V. Dych (New York, NY: Crossroad, 1978), 34.

It was confusing, terrifying, astounding; it was as though I was not really there but looking on from outside. I stood behind my mother's head, her firstborn. Her youngest child, my sister, stood at her feet—each of us on opposite ends of the body we had both come from, our consanguineous connection, the bridge between our beings. My brother and other sister had chosen not to come to the hospital for that final visit. But Paulette and I had and were now looking across at one another, unable to speak. We saw in each other's face the reality of what was to come. We were witnessing the end of things—and the beginning—thenceforth we were bound not only by ties of blood but by what cannot be measured or explained.

Death is most certainly a physical evil; the Apostle Paul writes of it in this way in his weighty Letter to the Romans and in his First Letter to the Corinthians. The fathers of the Second Vatican Council wrote that "It is in the face of death that the riddle of human existence grows most acute," describing the mystery of death as something that "utterly beggars the imagination."[4]

I know that the mystery of death is very close to the mystery of life, that they are intertwined. At twenty years of age most young adults in the industrialized, so-called developed world regard death as nothing but an indistinct, distant: it is a hazy galaxy far, far away. I've had a different notion from the age of twenty onward, before my complexion cleared of acne, before I was old enough to see the approaching end of my earthy being or that of other family members whose mortal lives have since concluded. This is God's will, God's inscrutable design. But there is also *my* will and *your* will. As a twenty-year-old I learned that we are creatures given the power to be unsure, to question. I look to the darkness in order to find the light. God is not death. But God can be found there, in that mystery that "beggars the imagination." I am as sure of this as I am sure of the spider that drowned in my shower when I tried to save it: a tiny black constellation plastered to the tiles, a tiny marker for the place where doubt and certainty intersect.

The horrific events reported in the newspaper clippings on my corkboard and my own intimate experience with death *could* potentially fit into a theodicy or philosophy I might find significant. But I don't want to go that route. It's not the way artists think when they're creating—at least not the way they *should* be thinking if what they're making is to possess any resonance.

I don't think about theodicy when I spot a news article about a particularly heinous act of human cruelty; I just cut it out and pin it to my corkboard. And I make no attempt to illuminate or elucidate some philosophy or theodicy while working

---

4. *Pastoral Constitution on the Church in the Modern World* (*Gaudium et Spes*), December 7, 1965, sec. 18.

on a story in which evil acts are portrayed and deaths occur. Fiction that does that is artificial. It doesn't ring true. In his essay "What Stories Are and Why We Read Them," Ron Hansen wrote that "Stories are not about theories or themes, though our high school practice of talking about books in this way often gives people the false impression that serious writers first of all have a point they're trying to prove." Said the late novelist Gilbert Sorrentino, "A writer discovers what he knows as he knows it, i.e., as he makes it. No artist writes in order to objectify an 'idea' already formed. It is the poem or novel or story that quite precisely tells him what he didn't know he knew: he knows, that is, only in terms of his writing. This is, of course, simply another way of saying that literary composition is not the placing of a held idea into a waiting form." Less verbose than Sorrentino, Flannery O'Connor said simply: "I write to discover what I know." In a 1956 letter to Eileen Hall, O'Connor also wrote, "Fiction is the concrete expression of mystery—mystery that is lived."[5]

I want to discover what I know about why stories of death and brutality so intrigue me—or anyone—by writing about those things, to attempt to discover why they possess such dark beauty and to see, by shaping lived mystery into form, where the path will lead. Gregory Wolfe, editor and publisher of *Image* journal, once remarked that in a good essay or poem or work of fiction it is neither the journey nor the arrival that matters, but the truth that lies somewhere in-between: "This is what I know so far."

This mysterious "in-between" resists definition and compartmentalization in the same way the news articles on my wall or the skull on my bookshelf resist definition. The fluid mystery of being cannot be forced into the logically circumscribed hole of philosophy or theodicy; if this happens, its beauty is lost, a beauty that sometimes rides a pale horse, or exists in the depiction of wild game on a kitchen counter in a sixteenth-century Flemish still life. Simone Weil wrote that "The sea is not less beautiful in our eyes because we know that ships are sometimes wrecked. On the contrary this adds to its beauty.... All the horrors which occur in this world are like the folds imposed upon the waves by gravity. That is why they contain an element of beauty."[6]

Rahner wrote that as creatures within creation we are participants in a great liturgy, an original and primary liturgy conjoined with history: "The world and its history are the terrible and sublime liturgy, breathing of death and sacrifice, which God celebrates and causes to be celebrated in and through human history in its freedom." The beauty of this terrible and sublime liturgy has at its heart the incomprehensible creative power of the divine: God the artist. But a ship lost at sea is one thing.

---

5. Hansen, *A Stay Against Confusion: Essays on Faith and Fiction* (New York, NY: HarperCollins, 2001), 33; Sorrentino, "The Act of Creation and Its Artifact," *Review of Contemporary Fiction* 19.3 (Fall 1999), 7; and O'Connor, *Flannery O'Connor: Spiritual Writings*, ed. Robert Ellsberg, Modern Spiritual Masters Series (Maryknoll, NY: Orbis Books, 2003), 130.

6. Weil, *Simone Weil*, 50.

A father microwaving his infant daughter is quite another. One possesses terrible beauty; the other possesses ugly banality. To quote Weil once again, "Imaginary evil is romantic and varied; real evil is gloomy, monotonous, barren, boring. Imaginary good is boring; real good is always new, marvelous, intoxicating. Therefore 'imaginative literature' is either boring or immoral (or a mixture of both). It only escapes from this alternative if in some way it passes over to the side of reality through the power of art."[7]

Weil can be cryptic and paradoxical and I will admit that I sometimes don't completely understand what she's saying. But the mystery she addresses calls for language that resists parsing, language that passes over to the side of reality. Real evil is indeed barren. Imaginary evil is varied because it has been fashioned in the furnace of the imagination, transformed into art. Art clothes our eyes in order that we may see the sublime in the death and sacrifice of the liturgy of the world we inhabit. We can sympathize with the mad and murderous through art. The scoundrels and scapegoats of art carry our iniquities into the wilderness and, extraordinarily, allow us to accompany them into the badlands and share in their affliction even while we despise them for their acts. Isn't it more interesting to read about the lost son who squanders his inheritance in dissipation and "loose living" only to find himself in the midst of a famine that has stricken the faraway land he inhabits? Isn't the prodigal son's decline, his misery in being reduced to a lowly swineherd who hungers for the fodder of the pigs he tends, more attention-grabbing and captivating than that of the elder son of Luke's parable? The elder son's story is dull. Imaginary good can be very boring indeed. I, for one, find the lost son a far more sympathetic character than the obedient son who stays at home.

O'Connor once wrote, "My own feeling is that writers who see by the light of their Christian faith will have, in these times, the sharpest eyes for the grotesque, for the perverse, and for the unacceptable."[8] The characters in my fiction tend toward those whose situations are grotesque and unacceptable, characters who are sometimes themselves perverse and who commit evil. They are the unfortunate and disadvantaged, the despised and despairing, individuals not completely in step with the world in which they must live.

The horrendous tales reported in the newspaper clippings on my corkboard are packets of unlabeled seeds. I sow them to see what species of grotesque flora come up, to see what swineherds and thugs and rapists and serial killers blossom. I cast them on the water in order to find them again, to discover what I know about the monsters that inhabit that beautiful, terrible sea that swallows ships. For I know not

---

7. Rahner, "Considerations on the Active Role of the Person in the Sacramental Event," in *Theological Investigations*, trans. David Bourke, vol. 14 (New York, NY: Seabury, 1976), 169; and Weil, *Gravity and Grace*, trans. Emma Craufurd (New York, NY: Routledge, 2002), 63.

8. O'Connor, *Flannery O'Connor*, 62.

what evil may happen on earth, and I know not how that evil is refashioned through the mysterious act of writing. I know only that by traveling with the scapegoat into the wilderness it is possible to glimpse the ineffable truth.

But what are scapegoats, exactly? And why do we hunger for them?

As I mentioned earlier, my desire to explore my thoughts on evil and death and beauty by simply writing about those things is difficult and complex. But René Girard maintains that there is a victimization process in all societies, a need for sacrificial victims who can be blamed for any crises a community faces, crises that threaten the established order and the community's peace. Paradoxically, the victim of this sacrifice—one usually chosen for his or her status as a person who lives on the margins of the community, someone who exhibits a recognizable degree of difference from the rest of the group—becomes not only the origin of the crisis but also the one who will redeem the community through his or her victimhood. This societal *scapegoat mechanism*, as Girard has termed it, turns the scapegoat—the despised—into a sacred victim by the peace he or she will restore.[9] This peace, however, is always temporary, always unstable. Violence begets violence. The scapegoat mechanism must be continuously repeated. The mob will eventually have to find another arbitrarily chosen person to blame, regardless of that person's guilt or innocence. In fact, the transgressions of the chosen scapegoat are usually either wildly exaggerated or completely invented. Referencing Girard, Kent State University English professor Gary Ciuba writes that "To avoid confronting how purely wanton is this murder, the community typically views its . . . victim as a monster deserving to be slaughtered. For if the actual randomness were acknowledged, the scapegoating would no longer work."[10]

There is much more to Girard's thought on sacred violence and the scapegoat mechanism, but suffice it to say, we all share in the tendency to make scapegoats of others, from gossip about an absent coworker in the break room to the trial and conviction of the West Memphis Three. Even Christians like myself, for whom the tradition of sacred violence was undermined and overturned by Jesus—someone who did not sanction violence and showed the scapegoat mechanism for the murder that it is by himself becoming scapegoated—even we are guilty of picking out individuals to blame for our own fears and anxieties. The insight of the Gospels, in which Christ's innocence is affirmed and sacred violence is turned inside out, is neglected, forgotten, or ignored. In his book *I See Satan Fall Like Lightning*, Girard writes that ". . . the

9. Girard, *The Scapegoat*, trans. Yvonne Freccero (Baltimore, MD: Johns Hopkins University Press, 1986).

10. Ciuba, *Desire, Violence, and Divinity in Modern Southern Fiction: Katherine Anne Porter, Flannery O'Connor, Cormac McCarthy, Walker Percy* (Baton Rouge, LA: Louisiana State University Press, 2007), 9.

biblical tradition punctures a universal delusion and reveals a truth never revealed before, the innocence not only of Jesus but of all similar victims."[11]

Still, we persist in our vicious blame game: he deserved it; she was a tramp; that boy wasn't right in the head. How can we confront this blame game and enter into an understanding of the victims of scapegoating, both the innocent and guilty? For those whose souls *aren't* inhabited by Christ—the overwhelming majority of us—art is one way of doing this.

As an example, I present Cormac McCarthy's 1973 novel *Child of God*, a tour de force of the protagonist as scapegoat and one of the darkest and most beautiful novels I've ever read (and have read over and over again). As readers, we accompany McCarthy's main character into the very bleakest depths of the wilderness. He is an utterly pitiable monster who we both despise and come to empathize with.

Set in eastern Tennessee during the early part of the twentieth century, *Child of God* is the story of Lester Ballard: a complete outcast forced to construct a reality that bears only the crudest and most elementary resemblance to the social body that has rejected him. Ballard is abandoned by his mother and orphaned by a father who hung himself, and his modest family land is auctioned off without his consent in a kind of celebration of Ballard's role as the community's scapegoat. Ballard then wanders Sevier County, alone and reviled. Though we readers can see the injustice of Ballard's predicament and are able to sympathize with him, we also see that he is absolutely repugnant. Ballard is a murderer and necrophile, an atrocious man-child cast out of a community he was never truly part of in the first place. But he is, as McCarthy writes at the very beginning of the novel, "A child of God much like yourself perhaps."[12]

O'Connor wrote that "It is when the freak can be sensed as a figure for our essential displacement that he attains some depth in literature." Lester Ballard is a freak. But he is also, as McCarthy insists on showing us, much like ourselves. As readers we try to deny Ballard by putting distance between ourselves and his monstrous actions. McCarthy does not allow us this distance, however, deftly manipulating reader response toward a kind of empathy with Ballard. This combination of repulsion and empathy is a blending of our comprehension of the vile things Ballard does and our recognition that he is *us*. Vereen Bell, in his excellent literary study *The Achievement of Cormac McCarthy*, writes that "Lester and his story are freakish and sensational, but they are worth attending because McCarthy has conceived pathetic Lester as a berserk version of fundamental aspects of ourselves—of our fear of time, our programmed infatuation with death, our loneliness, our threatening appetites, our narcissistic isolation from the world and the reality of other people."[13]

11. Girard, *I See Satan Fall Like Lightning*, trans. James G. Williams (Maryknoll, NY: Orbis Books, 2001), 1.
12. McCarthy, *Child of God* (New York, NY: Random House, 1973), 4.
13. O'Connor, *Mystery and Manners*, ed. Sally and Robert Fitzgerald (New York, NY: Farrar, Straus

An example of this comes at the opening of the middle portion of the novel, one that focuses completely on Ballard and chronicles his descent into necrophilia and madness. While coming off a mountain one winter morning after hunting squirrels, Ballard stumbles upon an asphyxiated couple in a still-running automobile, the car's windows fogged. The couple has apparently expired while having intercourse. Ballard turns off the ignition and rolls the body of the young man off the girl and onto the floor:

> The dead man was watching him from the floor of the car. Ballard kicked his feet out of the way and picked the girl's panties up from the floor and sniffed at them and put them in his pocket. He looked out the rear window and he listened. Kneeling there between the girl's legs he undid his buckle and lowered his trousers.
>
> A crazed gymnast laboring over a cold corpse. He poured into that waxen ear everything he'd ever thought of saying to a woman. Who could say she did not hear him?[14]

The scene is an utterly horrifying one, more for its portrayal of Ballard's loneliness and need for human companionship than for its appalling necrophilia. Says Bell: "In order for McCarthy to commend Lester to our attention and sympathy, it is necessary that he present Lester's story primarily from Lester's own point of view and that he show that his needs and behavior have at least vague affinities with our own."[15]

In the course of the novel, Ballard collects the corpses of those he's killed along with stuffed animals won at a county fair shooting gallery. He clings to them tenaciously, even buying clothing for a girl whose body he transports to an abandoned house, storing the carcass in the attic when he is not talking to it or posing it in front of a fire built in the house's old fireplace.

McCarthy renders scenes like these unrelentingly: scenes of murder and incest, the recounting of an 1899 hanging in which townsfolk sleep in their wagons and have picnics on the courthouse lawn in anticipation of the gruesome event. In a scene in which Ballard brings a half-frozen robin as a present for the hydrocephalic toddler of a woman he's interested in, the child chews the bird's legs off. McCarthy infuses these scenes with elements that call attention to the fact that Ballard is "A child of God much like yourself perhaps." Writes Gary Ciuba: "Although the violence of reading *Child of God* is first felt in the shock that separates Ballard and the reader, an even more surprising form of fictional assault is the way that the novel works to undermine precisely this fundamental difference. McCarthy does not allow readers to take

---

& Giroux, 1997), 45; and Bell, *The Achievement of Cormac McCarthy* (Baton Rouge, LA: Louisiana State University Press, 1988), 55.

14. McCarthy, *Child of God*, 88–89.
15. Bell, *The Achievement of Cormac McCarthy*, 65.

high-toned refuge in condemning a miscreant who is obviously unrelated to them. Rather, he suggests an unexpected kinship..."[16]

Ballard is so pathologically disconnected from the world and the community that has scapegoated him that he eventually comes to occupy a mountain cave with the bodies of his victims and his toy carnival animals. McCarthy describes it as not so much a place of habitation as the interior space of a living organism: "Here the walls with their softlooking convolutions, slavered over as they were with wet and bloodred mud, had an organic look to them, like the innards of some great beast. Here in the bowels of the mountain Ballard turned his light on ledges or pallets of stone where dead people lay like saints."[17]

Ballard resides under the earth because he is not welcome on its surface. He lurks under Sevier County, Tennessee, like a cancerous polyp whose living death is represented by the subterranean but who is also sacred and saintly for the function he serves as the community's scapegoat. As readers, we are there with him, fellow scapegoats exiled to the grave by a population wishing to cleanse itself of the things it knows itself to be.

It is only when Ballard physically dies that he becomes a member of the community that banished him to a living death; existing only as a productive member of society when he becomes an object of science, his body is shipped to a medical school to be thoroughly dissected and examined by students. His remains are "scraped from the table into a plastic bag and taken with others of his kind to a cemetery outside the city and there interred. A minister from the school read a simple service."[18] As the sacrificial victim Ballard is holy: he is shown a modicum of respect by being honored with a humble funeral. And we, the readers, are both in attendance at that service and the ones who join Ballard in his interment.

There is beauty in this. Apart from McCarthy's exquisitely baroque style and masterful craftsmanship, there is beauty in the fact that the darkness he portrays is depicted with such finesse and visual richness. And there is beauty in the way he keeps us engaged not only as spectators but also as Lester Ballard's fellow travelers. We are scapegoated along with Ballard; we are able to better understand his plight and ours. *We* deserve it. *We* are the tramp. *We* are the boy not right in the head.

"To project one's being into an afflicted person," wrote Simone Weil, "is to assume for a moment his affliction, it is to choose voluntarily something whose very essence consists in being imposed by constraints upon the unwilling. And that is an

---

16. Ciuba, *Desire, Violence, and Divinity*, 189–90.
17. McCarthy, *Child of God*, 135.
18. Ibid., 194.

impossibility. Only Christ has done it. Only Christ and those men whose soul he possesses can do it."[19]

"Witnesses describe brutal beating on country road."

"Police, family, hope for tips in teen girl's 'horrific' slaying."

"Chilling testimony in trial of roofer charged with torture, murder."

"Man found guilty of drowning three-year-old stepdaughter for insurance money."

"Ohio cult leader executed for murdering family of four."

"Police arrest teenage mother of dead newborn."

I've told you about my corkboard and the newspaper clippings pinned to it, evidence of the ontological reality of evil and its twin, the reality of death, things I see every morning while doing the dishes, a merging of the mundane and the mysterious. I've told you that we despise the scapegoats we create. I've told you that by accompanying the scapegoat into the wilderness we might appreciate him or her in unexpected ways.

There are sunken ships and stillborn infants and executed convicts braided into a garland of flowers draped from the goat's horns, a blossoming of beauty amid affliction, terrible and sublime. This is what I know so far.

---

19. Weil, *Simone Weil*, 63.

7 Burning Dog

by MARK FLEMING

THE BOY WAS SUSPENDED from school for three days, and on the third day he spied a cat through a downstairs window. It was curled up on the patio sofa in back. He'd seen it before—gray with dark swirls—tailing a lady walking her foo-foo dog. Right up the middle of the street, it followed them. Carried itself like a little lion.

The boy went upstairs and got a lighter and a bottle of cooking oil. He'd almost left the kitchen when he stopped, thought, and went back for a can of tuna. He opened the can, pressed the lid to drain the liquid.

Downstairs, the boy opened the patio door. The cat watched him and flicked its tail. Beneath the low thick overcast, its yellow eyes were huge.

"Get a whiff of this," the boy said, holding out the can. The cat's eyes got bigger as the boy got closer, but it didn't run. "Nice kitty," the boy said, looking around before he sat on the sofa. He set the bottle next to his leg. The cat stretched and looked at him like he was supposed to pet it. It didn't seem to care about the tuna, so the boy set aside the can.

The other backyards were empty. Everyone was at work. Nobody would miss the cat, except possibly the person who'd put the blue collar on it. He held his hand above the cat and waited. The cat closed its eyes. He stroked its fur, which was soft and sleek. It purred.

The cat felt fragile. With one hand he could fling it against the brick.

The boy had been suspended for decking another seventh grader, a fuckface who'd said "kissy, kissy" to him. In the principal's office afterward, the boy had refused to say why that had made him angry. He wouldn't repeat the story that fuckface must've heard.

The story was this: When the boy was in fourth grade, there was a popular second grader with blond hair as long as a girl's. Both boys were in the after-school program, so they were on the playground at the same time. Everyone was playing tag, and the boy was it. He caught and tackled the second grader. Their faces accidentally touched.

"Stop kissing me!" the second grader had shouted.

"Kissy, kissy," everyone had teased.

The boy had run, though that was the last time. Later that year, his father had moved out, and the boy had put on weight. At the end of fifth grade, he would've been held back, but the teachers couldn't wait for him to move on to middle school.

He stopped petting the cat to pour a little oil onto one palm. After rubbing his hands together, he drew them one after the other along the length of the cat's tail. He'd seen his mother do this with a client's arms. She'd put the oil in a squeeze bottle and scent it with lavender. He put more oil on his hands. The tail curled against his hand with each pull.

When the tail was soaked, the boy wiped his hands on the cat's body. Again he checked the neighbors' back windows. Then with one hand he seized the cat's neck and pressed it into the seat cushion. Snarling and squirming, it clawed his forearm. The boy slid off the sofa. He had trouble connecting the lighter to the tail, but it caught and went up like a torch. He let go.

The cat ran from hiding spot to hiding spot like it could outrun its burning tail. It would run, stop in a crouch, run again.

"Stop, drop, and roll, fuckface!" the boy yelled. The cat ran into the woods between the houses and the beltway. The boy scanned for witnesses, but there was nothing but smoke and the smell of burned hair.

He pinched tuna from the can. That cat wouldn't come around again. Munching on the tuna, he went inside to stop the bleeding from the scratches.

Though the neighbor was no weakling, JJ was crazy strong. The dog dragged him down the street from For Rent sign to telephone pole to For Sale sign to fire hydrant. He hoped his neighbors didn't see the mutt hauling him along. He was seventy-six.

"Whoa, boy," he told JJ. "Heel."

JJ tugged and panted, nails scratching against the pavement. His long black coat, like a Belgian Shepherd's, had to be hot even on a gray spring afternoon. But JJ loved going out in all kinds of weather. He loved every dog or human that he saw. He ran on pure dumb affection.

JJ stopped to investigate another dog's calling card, and the neighbor relaxed. The dog belonged to his granddaughter who'd just finished college. Her first real apartment didn't allow dogs over fifteen pounds, so the hunt had been on for a caretaker. That is, a softhearted sucker—Grandpa.

"He won't be too much for you, will he?" his granddaughter had asked on the day she'd dropped JJ off. No one in the family would've asked this a year ago.

"No, no," he'd said. "I'll have him shipshape in no time." What else could he say? His granddaughter was having trouble letting go of the dog's neck.

And although JJ was male, he squatted like a bitch.

Ahead on the street, a teenage boy in a T-shirt and baggy pants practiced skateboarding, and the dog charged straight for him. The boy was flipping the skateboard in circles beneath his feet and trying to land back on it. His droopy dungarees weren't helping. When the boy noticed the dog, he stomped on one end of the skateboard, tipping it up into his hands and raising it like a bat. There were ugly red scratches on his arm.

"It's all right," the neighbor called. "What you're doing just looks like fun to him." He would've steered JJ to the opposite side of the street, but the dog had other intentions, and it hurt the neighbor's chest to resist. He managed to halt JJ a few feet from the boy. His tail wagging to beat the band, the dog exhibited such friendliness that the boy lowered the skateboard and looked uncertainly from JJ to the neighbor.

Now the neighbor recognized the boy as the one his wife had predicted was "sadly headed for prison." This was last spring, when she was battling cancer. She spent her remaining days lying on the couch, looking out the bay window in front. On the street, the boy had been riding a pink bike back and forth.

"Another delinquent," the neighbor had said then. He would've marched out to set him straight on a couple of things, as he'd done with neighborhood boys in the past, but he didn't want to leave his wife.

"They leased the house four doors up," she'd said. "I don't think he gets enough supervision."

The delinquent, laughing, had raced off with the bike when a girl had come running for it, but here he was again, hanging out on the curb when he should be in school. Still, the bike incident seemed like distant history.

"He's not going to bite?" the boy asked.

"Let him smell your hand and more than likely he'll knock you over and lick you to death," he said.

Tucking the skateboard under his arm, the boy extended his other hand.

"Just don't make any sudden movements. He gets excited and nips, thinking you're playing."

JJ strained at the leash, tongue lolling.

"He's got big teeth," the boy said, withdrawing his hand slightly.

"His name's JJ," the neighbor said. "Don't ask what that stands for. Probably something your age would know about. He's my granddaughter's."

At last the boy's hand was close enough to sniff. The neighbor thought JJ might growl, shrink back, but true to form, he lapped the boy's fingers as if they were covered in meat juice.

The boy just stood there.

"You can pet him," the neighbor said. "Go ahead, scratch behind his ears." JJ's eyes followed the boy's hand as it came around. But as soon as the boy started to scratch, the dog sat next to the curb and cocked his head to better show off the spot behind his ears.

"Nice to meet you," the neighbor said, offering his hand to the boy. His grip would tell him everything.

"My dad had two boxers," the boy replied, ignoring the neighbor. "He was going to breed them. They could tear anything to pieces."

The neighbor put his hand in his pocket. "The boxer is a beautiful dog."

"My mom worried they'd hurt me cause I was little at the time. She took them and let them loose in the country." He stopped petting JJ and looked toward his house. "Thousands of dollars in dog, gone like that." He snapped his fingers.

JJ jerked his head toward the sound.

The neighbor heard the father speaking through the son. No doubt the boy's father had been a delinquent, too.

The boy dropped the skateboard, stepped on it, kicked off.

JJ lunged in pursuit, and the neighbor was yanked to his hands and knees. The pavement ripped into his palms, tore holes in his trousers. JJ barked and whined and struggled against the leash.

The boy looked back and grinned. "Who's walking who?" he shouted. He didn't stop.

The boy searched the woods for the cat. He smoked a cigarette and carried the oil bottle. He wanted to see its charred body and destroy the evidence. He wanted that blue collar. But the woods were thick with underbrush and vines, discarded mattresses and tires. He didn't see burnt leaves or anything marking the cat's path. The cat could be anywhere, and someone might look out a window and see him. He'd finish another cigarette and turn back.

A shaggy black dog barked at him from behind a four-foot-high chain-link fence. JJ—the stupid dog with ADD. The dog stood on his back legs, front paws on the top rail. He wanted out.

"Hey, JJ," the boy said, looking up at the house. The windows were dark. He exited the trees, sliding the bottle into his back pocket. "Hey, boy, remember me?" He reached out and the dog licked his fingers.

"You want to come out and play? You can help me find that crispy-fried cat." But the gate was too close to the house. "Sorry, pup." The boy flicked away his cigarette and started back into the woods.

Something moved through the woods behind him. He feared it was the cat, but when he turned, JJ leaped on him and knocked him over, licking his face.

"OK, OK!" the boy said, trying to push the dog off. He laughed. "I give up." He got to his feet and could see the dog was eager for more. "You just love to play," the boy told him in a baby voice. "Don't you?"

JJ panted and appeared to be smiling.

The boy feinted left and the dog followed. The boy turned left and ran. At once the dog was at his legs, barking. He feinted right, ran, throwing off the dog for only a second. JJ chased him and the boy chased JJ. They chased each other through the woods back to the boy's house.

He brought out a bowl of water for JJ and set it on the patio. As JJ slobbered it up, the boy sat and petted him. The hair behind his ears was fuzzier than on his back and sides. He had dark nails, long hairs where his dick would come out. The boy felt muscles, hard as knots, under the wiry hair. There was nothing fragile about this dog.

JJ lay down, still drinking from the bowl.

"You were thirsty, weren't you?"

The boy took the bottle from his pocket and rubbed oil between his hands. JJ watched and went back to drinking. The boy drew his hands along JJ's tail like he did with the cat, like one girl gathering another's ponytail. And just like the cat, JJ didn't seem to mind. But JJ had a lot more hair. It soaked up the oil and remained rough to the touch.

"It's that heavy coat of yours," the boy said, putting more oil on his hands.

JJ got to his feet, stretched, and stood next to the boy. The dog panted but otherwise looked rested and ready for more play. The boy worked his way from the tail to JJ's back. He applied more oil and ran his hands along JJ's spine. He ran them down JJ's legs.

"You like that, don't you?" the boy said.

JJ licked the boy's face.

The boy took out his lighter and flicked it. JJ was fascinated. Everywhere the boy moved the flame, JJ's gaze followed. With JJ watching, the boy held the lighter to the hair on the dog's hind leg.

It smoldered but didn't catch. JJ didn't budge. The boy flicked the lighter again. This time he snagged JJ's tail and held the flame to its tip. Only smoke. The boy let go and JJ wagged it, tracing smoke Zs. JJ kept his eyes on the lighter.

The boy put away the lighter and scratched behind the dog's ears. "You're indestructible."

The boy sat with the dog, looking out on the woods and the beltway. Beyond the trees, cars raced by. Maybe the neighbor would let him keep the dog. The boy could control him, whereas the old guy obviously couldn't.

JJ's tail burst into flames.

The boy jerked, which made JJ jerk and knock over the oil bottle, splashing it on the boy. He jumped up. His pant leg was on fire. In shock, he walked toward the backyard with his elbows lifted as if he were wading into a lake. JJ tagged along, his tail a waving torch. He still wanted to play. The boy fell to the grass. There was immediate relief. He rolled and rolled to stop the burn.

Delighted with the game, JJ pounced on the boy over and over, rekindling the flame.

Earlier, the neighbor had put JJ in the backyard and limped inside. If the dog got out again, so be it. What was his granddaughter doing with a dog in college, anyhow? At the kitchen sink, the neighbor dabbed the grit from his wounds with a wet dishcloth. Had his wife been there, she would've fussed all over him. And if the kids found out, he'd never hear the end of it: sell the house and live with one of us, they'd say. Yet his granddaughter sure loved that dog. He applied iodine, wincing at the sting because no one would see. His heart thumped: too fast. He took one of his pills and limped to the couch to lie down. He should have let go of that leash.

JJ started barking.

Damn dog. Let the dog chase the boy. That's what dogs do. That's what boys do, even budding psychopaths.

But he'd held on. His wife had always said he was stubborn, and it had cost him plenty—he'd outlived her. "It should've been me," he said. He teared up. On top of everything, his pills turned him into a crybaby. JJ stopped barking and the neighbor dozed off.

He woke with a snort. He'd been snoring. Now JJ's bark had a higher pitch. The neighbor thought he heard a human cry. He shook off the nap and limped to the window.

A boy toppled over the back fence and a dog leaped it. It was the boy from the street, and from the waist down he was on fire. What the hell? The boy staggered toward the house. Flames also rose from JJ's back, fluttered with each wag of his tail. JJ jumped on the boy and the boy pushed him off. The boy fell and then climbed to his feet. Again JJ jumped on the boy and the boy pushed him off. "Down!" the boy screamed. JJ jumped again.

"Help! Help!"

The neighbor grabbed the blanket from the couch and, limp gone, started downstairs to the back door. In the Coast Guard, he'd witnessed a deck fire and he knew both would suffer terrible burns, but he could save one, and there was no question which one he would choose.

8 Evil Is What Humans Do: An Interview with Christian Wiman

by ALLISON BACKOUS

CHRISTIAN WIMAN IS THE editor of *Poetry* magazine, the author of several poetry and essay collections, and a revered contributor to such prestigious publications as the *Harvard Divinity Bulletin* and the *New Yorker*. His forthcoming book, *My Bright Abyss: Meditations of a Modern Believer*, explores the central themes of his work, including frailty, illness, and the love of God. In this interview, Wiman discusses his work, his attention to lament and evil, and his perspective concerning the role of spirituality in contemporary American poetry.

The Other Journal (TOJ): I've spent the past year reading your essay "Gazing into the Abyss" from the Summer 2007 issue of the *American Scholar*, and it is one of the best apologetics I've read for poetry and a spiritual life. What brought you to put this essay together? What do you have to say about it now?

Christian Wiman (CW): I've had a handful of essays in my life that came to me as poems—that is to say, they just came. That particular essay was written at a period of real crisis. I had just been diagnosed with cancer, and the news I was getting from various doctors in Chicago and elsewhere made my situation seem very dire. And yet I didn't feel dire, at least not absolutely. I felt, as I say in the essay, abradingly alive, an effect of being in love with the world and one woman and the life that it seemed I was going to lose.

TOJ: In that essay, you consider several passages from Simone Weil, who happens to be a long favorite of mine—what other passages of her work speak to you?

CW: I've always been bowled over by these lines: "We must take the feeling of being home into exile. / We must be rooted in the absence of a place." For many years, this seemed to perfectly articulate the dynamic in which I found myself, and it gave me a way to think of that dynamic in positive terms rather than negative ones. I also love "He who has not experienced the presence of God cannot feel his absence," which led me to say at the end of one of my own essays "I never truly felt the pain of unbelief until I began to believe."[1]

TOJ: I taught *Every Riven Thing* to my writing students last fall, and I was surprised that a group of evangelical Christian youth not only identified closely with the book but that they followed its forms so well. What has surprised or challenged you about people's responses to the book?[2]

CW: I have not been surprised by what you might call the "religious" responses to the book, only because I think there is a hunger in this country right now—even among people who would call themselves evangelicals—for an art that speaks to people at, well, the level of art. There's not much out there, and most of it comes from unbelievers. As for following the forms, that does surprise (and delight) me!

In the more secular literary world where I live, some people have not had such a warm response to the so-called religious content in the book. Clive James, in an otherwise positive review, said that those particular poems were the worst in the book. James is an atheist, though, which may explain that response. Or maybe those poems really are the worst in the book. Who knows! That is not for me to say. All I know is that I had to write them.[3]

TOJ: I hear so much lament in *Every Riven Thing*, lament over the possibilities of impending loss. How do the ideas of lament and evil connect or rub against each other for you?

CW: I just read a passage from the poet Eleanor Wilner the other day in which she said that protest and lament could also be forms of praise. I agree completely. Yes, there is a lot of lament in *Every Riven Thing*, but I feel in my bones that it is, ultimately,

---

1. Weil, *A Simone Weil Reader*, ed. George A. Panichas (New York, NY: McKay, 1977), 356; Weil quoted in Wiman, *Ambition and Survival: Becoming a Poet* (Port Townsend, WA: Copper Canyon Press, 2007), 138; and Wiman, "My Bright Abyss," *American Scholar*, Winter 2009, http://theamericanscholar.org/my-bright-abyss/.

2. Wiman, *Every Riven Thing: Poems* (New York, NY: Farrar, Straus and Giroux, 2011).

3. See James, "Rocket Man," review of *Every Riven Thing: Poems*, by Christian Wiman, *Financial Times*, November 12, 2010, http://www.ft.com/intl/cms/s/2/b755fae4-ede9-11df-8616-00144feab49a.html#axzz1o6o2HgxC.

a book of praise and joy. After all, the Psalms are full of lament. The whole Bible is full of lament.[4]

I know that many people link evil and illness—including, disappointingly, Jesus—but I find the idea either benighted or offensive. Little kids get cancer. Babies get cancer. Were they being evil? Evil is what humans do, not some judgment visited upon them for what they have done.

TOJ: You wrote "The Limit" ten years ago, and I hear some significant differences in your approaches to pain and to personal narrative in your span of work since then. Do you hear this? Or do you hear something else?[5]

CW: I have much more hope and fullness of spirit than when I wrote "The Limit," though that essay was itself an attempt to find my way to those things. I do hear a great difference in my work over the past ten years, which (I hope!) has gone from relying wholly on emptiness and absence as fuel for art to including experiences of abundance and joy. The difference, in a word, though there is no word, is *God*.

TOJ: Is it still true that "pain may be its own reprieve," as you wrote in "The Limit"? It reminds me of the poem "One Time," in which you wrote "praise to the pain scalding us towards each other." Do these two lines resonate with each other still for you?[6]

CW: That's a very interesting connection and one I hadn't thought of. The lines do resonate with each other, though they are also very different. The first is enclosed and deeply informed by Simone Weil, whose thinking, though brilliant, has real limitations. The second leads to a "beyond": it is not simply a reprieve but a release into some fulfillment and grace.

---

4. See Wilner et al., "One Whole Voice," *Poetry*, February 2012, http://www.poetryfoundation.org/poetrymagazine/article/243400.

5. See Wiman, "The Limit," *Threepenny Review* 87 (2001): http://www.threepennyreview.com/samples/wiman_f01.html.

6. Wiman, "One Time," in *Every Riven Thing*, 29.

9 Open Your Eyes Wide:
The Generous Vision of Marilynne Robinson

by REBECCA MARTIN

Marilynne Robinson. *When I Was a Child I Read Books*. New York, NY: Farrar, Straus, and Giroux, 2012.

IN MARILYNNE ROBINSON'S NOVEL *Gilead*, the Reverend John Ames observes that "you never do know the actual nature even of your own experience"—much less that of others.[1] In her new essay collection, *When I Was a Child I Read Books*, Robinson applies the idea with rigor. There is "sacred mystery with every individual experience, every life," she says (xiv). In view of that mystery, we must "forget definition, forget assumption, watch" (7).

These essays are not for the faint of heart. Readers of her novels will find some of the unhurried pace and lyrical prose they expect, but only those familiar with her past essays will be unsurprised at her incisive, pointed language and depth of argument. Both kinds of readers, however, will recognize consistency in her views of humanity and culture. In all her writing, Robinson calls for stepping back, gauging circumstances with an outsider's gaze, and then acting in love toward others. "When we accept dismissive judgments for our community," she says, "we stop having generous hopes for it" (30). Dismissive judgment is not something Robinson will allow; generous hope is not something she will cede.

These are ideas that Robinson has been developing for several decades. In her early novel *Housekeeping*, life is experienced in new and unexpected ways by characters who live outside the boundaries of traditional American expectations. The

---

1. Robinson, *Gilead* (New York, NY: Farrar, Straus and Giroux, 2004), 95.

more recent Pulitzer Prize–winning *Gilead* and its companion novel, *Home*, are an experiment in otherness, as the characters learn, or don't learn, to move beyond their assumptions of each other. In her nonfiction, Robinson approaches these same ideas with an unapologetic directness. Her initial collection, *The Death of Adam*, and her more recent *Absence of Mind* develop her imperative that we must rethink what we think we know. Even her *Mother Country: Britain, the Welfare State, and Nuclear Pollution*, which at first glance seems substantially different from her other work, is a call to look at a difficult situation with new eyes.

Robinson is well suited to seeing things from many sides. She is a child of the American West, which she celebrates for its outsider identity. She has been deeply influenced by the civil rights movement and its upheaval of so many prescriptions, assumptions, and expectations. She knows what it is to be an outsider within her own academic community, as well; she not only confesses a Christian faith that is strongly Calvinistic, but, in her analyses of society and culture, she often arrives at a uniquely liberal stance by means of that Calvinism's very tenets. And she is an unapologetic historian; her knowledge of many histories and literatures plays a large role in, as she says, her "perspective on this civilization" (xiv). She approaches her topics from a position of sociohistorical awareness that cultivates an openhanded generosity to experiences different than her own.

Now Robinson's careful, calculated vantage informs her new collection, as she brings a broad historical perspective to bear on her critique of entrenched American social, political, and cultural ideologies. In these ten essays, some previously published, some new, Robinson looks again to the past for instruction as she addresses the dangers of assumption. In the first several essays, she considers such modern concerns as education, the religion-versus-science debate, and American capitalist culture. In "Open Thy Hand Wide," she melds political critique with biblical criticism, exploring the connection between a Calvinistic liberalism and the development of America's social thought, and after the title essay, she discusses Old Testament law, the gospel of Christ as narrative, and the role of religion in determining human rights. Even so, her application always turns to modern culture, with very practical and pointed implications for a political climate that NPR described as vicious and polarized.[2] Throughout, Robinson's Calvinist faith and history together provide the lens through which she even-mindedly perceives such pressing issues as religious patriotism, government assistance, and the evolution of modern science.

Then there is the title essay. It is no accident that "When I Was a Child" is identified as central to the collection. There, Robinson gets personal and grows more lyrical as she recalls her childhood landscape. History and economics and modern culture

---

2. Linton Weeks, "The Slimary Process: Is This The Nastiest Race Ever?," NPR, January 31, 2012, http://www.npr.org/2012/01/31/146080015/the-slimary-process-is-this-the-nastiest-race-ever.

still find their way in. This is, after all, an essay about the American West, but it is also about Robinson and her home. And what she appreciates about her Idaho upbringing is the loneliness it fostered, the intellectual clarity that came by way of a solitary education: "I think it was in fact peculiarly Western to feel no tie of particularity to any single past or history, to experience . . . the meditative, free appreciation of whatever comes under one's eye" (85). The result is a singular individuality that is beautiful, near sacred. Amid a culture that has lost the capacity to question itself, the benefit of this outsider position is that it provides a clearer perspective on self and others. This, in turn, enables a posture of humble generosity, both intellectual and material. If this entire collection is the outworking of Robinson's philosophy of "looking at things from a little distance," this essay explains how that outsider identity developed in her (90).

From a critique of finance economics to a description of the library she frequented as a child, it is no small feat that Robinson's topics are both expansive and precise. And it is not unintentional. In these essays, her inquisitive, inductive stance expands out into the cosmos and deep into the warring history of the world. She begins her critique of modern capitalism, of all things, with a meditation on the planet Mercury, pondering the universe's vastness as a telescopic view to the value of individual human life. "Say that we are a puff of warm breath in a very cold universe. By this kind of reckoning we are either immeasurably insignificant or we are incalculably precious and interesting" (36). This perspective that is both broad and personal illuminates the value of putting ourselves in others' shoes, whoever that "other" may be: Stalin or Churchill, Cold War Russia or present-day China, colonial Puritans or the unknown neighbor in need. In international relations, in understanding ourselves, always graciousness and objectivity—"Indeed, graciousness might be the most valuable consequence of objectivity" (44). The world is full of glories, mysteries, ambiguities, and, according to Robinson's Christianity, sin. And so the "straight-edge ruler" of clear-cut, simplistic answers based on entrenched ideologies will not work (49). She surmises that when we are able to step outside of ourselves and hold others in sympathetic imagination, we will care for each other in a way that sustains culture and betters the world.

This concept of imaginative sympathy is deeply rooted in Robinson's faith. And it is at the unexpected convergence of her faith and her politics that she grows most emphatic and unyielding. It would be easy to pigeonhole Robinson based on her theological standing, and she, of course, addresses that. She confesses the Bible and the gospel of Christ; she identifies herself as a Calvinist. Since Calvinism was the purview of the Puritans, it is easy to think of those more exacting American founders as harsh or unjust, but Robinson is quick to identify those notions as preconceived. In one of the essays, she reconsiders the Puritan faith as particularly lenient and generous. She details the Old Testament laws that make provision for those in need: "Thou shalt open thy hand unto thy brother, to thy nedie, and to thy poore in the land" (68). And she clarifies that Old Testament and Puritan punishments, especially those for crimes committed out of poverty and need, were far more just and fitting to the crime than those in later history, or even in America today. It is only assumptions that have led us to think otherwise. The Calvinist faith, in fact, prompted our forebears, as it might prompt us, to a more-than-equitable dealing with others. She quotes John Calvin: "The Lord makes them truly kind and bountiful, so that they no longer seek their own convenience, but are ready to give assistance to the poor, and not only do this once or oftener, but every day advance more and more in kindness and generosity" (67).

Consequently, Robinson's brand of Calvinist faith leads to a strikingly liberal and humanist response. One pervasive strain of American thought says we own what we earn. Robinson looks back to the beginnings of American history and deeply into Calvinist theology and finds a contrasting perspective. According to Thomas Jefferson, every human being is sacred, and justice is a right that should be given to all, not earned by some; according to the likes of Calvin, the best way to live is to hold our belongings with an open hand. And so Robinson approves responses like government funding for the poor: "In my Bible, Jesus does *not* say, 'I was hungry and you fed me, though not in such a way as to interfere with free-market principles.'" (139). She urges Americans to set aside narrow notions of individual gain. She hopes we might instead be willing to sympathetically imagine and understand the circumstances of others, thus moving toward a liberal care for each other, even to a sacrificial degree. Her essays are an exercise in perspective.

It isn't always easy going. To say these essays require a close reading would be an understatement. As in her other nonfiction, Robinson's writing style is as complex as her theological and political views. She has a syntactic tendency to shift between opposing ideas, and she depends on the reader to make the proper distinctions and interpretations. And the density of her arguments, alongside some very specific topics and references—capitalist ideology, for example, or World War II history—may lose some who prefer the simpler, contained worlds of Gilead or Fingerbone. Robinson also seems to make some assumptions herself about her readers' previous knowledge of, say, John Winthrop or Sigmund Freud or a host of other historical theologians, classical philosophers, and Puritan preachers. This is a compliment to the reader. Robinson's prose might be dense, but it is shot through with a radiance that reflects a glorious hope for humanity, all the while applying an invigorating reason.

In her essays, as in her fiction, Robinson is comfortable taking time and care to develop her arguments. Her essays must be read with patience, taking in all the information, waiting for what will surely come: the grand climax of her strong, incisive response. There is no trickery here, just a premium placed on considering all the sides, or at least many of them, before making a judgment. The book's very title echoes Paul in 1 Corinthians 13: "When I was a child, I spoke like a child, I thought like a child, I reasoned like a child." He goes on: "When I became a man, I gave up childish ways." Robinson reminds us that we "know only in part" (1 Cor. 13:11–12 ESV). And so she presents a grown-up approach to thinking about other people and about the governance of them. It is a mature, informed, and fair-minded approach. Her final conclusions are resolute, but they are arrived at by way of careful consideration.

In *Gilead*, *Home*, and *Housekeeping*, Robinson tells and retells stories of gracious forgiveness and love, and she personifies that lonely, living landscape of the American West. All of these threads are woven throughout *When I Was a Child I Read Books*. The result is a pervasive theme of perceptive, hopeful generosity, whether considering Stalin's position in World War I, Charles Finney's abolitionism in the mid-1800s, or the poor and needy in America today. Robinson's social critique is direct and sometimes bracing, but her theology and her patriotism are actively optimistic.

To be fair, *Gilead*'s Reverend Ames does not always practice the grace—that is, the approach from an admitted lack of understanding—that he preaches. Against all Robinson's advice, he makes fear-based assumptions about others. He demonstrates endless understanding toward his closest friends and family, but when adversity comes in the form of his best friend's profligate son, he assumes the worst about the young man's meanings and intentions. Still, he is growing. "Wherever you turn your eyes the world can shine like transfiguration," he says. "You don't have to bring a thing to it except a little willingness to see."[3] That is Robinson's hope for us all. When faulty assumptions are put aside, "we are instructed in the endless brilliance of creation" (11). It is no small hope.

---

3. Robinson, *Gilead*, 245.

10 Bleakness and Richness: Christopher Nolan on Human Nature

by LAUREN WILFORD

I REMEMBER THE FRENETIC BUZZING in my head on the way out of the midnight showing of *The Dark Knight*. I remember the way the theater seemed to heave after the final frame, all at once ringing with cheers, expletives, arguments, and the laughter of release. We went home and made all our friends see it. We watched the box office numbers climb like we had money on them.

As part of the millennial generation, I've seen my fair share of franchise mania—people always want to talk about the latest Spider-Man or Harry Potter—but people wanted to *talk* about *The Dark Knight* at a level I had never seen before. By the time the film opened, Christopher Nolan had already released five films as a director and cowriter—three noir-influenced crime dramas, his first Batman film, and a period thriller—to increasing acclaim and financial success. All were dark and philosophically bent. But none of those films had generated its own cultural moment.

Part of this fervor was related to the well-deserved hype concerning Heath Ledger's penultimate performance. Remember how gleeful we felt to meet Johnny Depp's Jack Sparrow? Watching Ledger's Joker took that feeling to dizzy, depraved heights. From the second he walked into the frame with his deadpan laugh and matted hair, we were rapt. By three lines in ("I'm gonna make this pencil—disappear"), the audience had lost it. It was the most literally I have ever sat on the edge of my seat. It was the first time I had laughed and gasped in the same breath. Ledger's Joker made the film a ride.

Mere rides don't linger, though, and *The Dark Knight* lingered.

Comic book films arrive weighted with moral symbolism—they pit good against evil with colored capes to serve as team markers. *Superman* gave us sturdy metaphors: a Christ figure, kryptonite, Metropolis. *Spider-Man*'s Green Goblin had a few Nietzschean sermons for our bug-bitten everyman. But director and cowriter Christopher Nolan's experience with hard-boiled crime films lent *The Dark Knight* a moral gravity that refused to be ignored. Its characters discussed ancient Roman dictators over dinner. Its villain was terrifying, but the film also pondered the frightening possibilities inside its heroes. And a few of its ethically fraught episodes were insomnia worthy.

No scene is as provocative as the ferry scene. The setup is this: the psychopathic Joker has rigged two ferries with explosives. One boat carries civilians and one, criminals. The Joker then gives each ferry the detonator to the other boat's bombs and claims that if neither ferry has destroyed the other by midnight, he will destroy both of them. It's the classic utilitarian dilemma spiked with authority issues—can we discard some lives in order to spare others? Are there scenarios where it makes sense to agree to a terrorist's terms? Who makes the decisions?

The results of this experiment are maddening to anyone looking for a straightforward lesson on human nature. The civilians vote three-to-one for destroying the other ferry, but no individual is willing to engage the detonator. The criminals take no vote; their choice is made by a strong-willed leader who throws the detonator out the window. Neither destroys the other, and for that, the Joker seems to have failed in his thesis: "When the chips are down, these civilized people, they'll eat each other."

They don't eat each other. But they wanted to. So who won?

This is the type of question repeatedly invoked in *The Dark Knight* and, indeed, throughout Nolan's dark body of work. Perhaps the decision to make "Why so serious?" into the Joker's sinister catchphrase was arch—for it is precisely Nolan's seriousness that made the film so wildly successful. The Joker is more than a villain—he is a force of nature, "a dog chasing cars," nihilism embodied. Batman is repeatedly characterized as a shadowy symbol, as "more than a hero." When they face off, ideas hang in the balance, and we can feel the urgency. Batman deals blows to a Joker who merely laughs; it's justice versus chaos, Batman's unstoppable force meeting the Joker's immovable object.

But *The Dark Knight* resists moralizing. It is not just an allegory or clash of the ideological titans. There are archetypes here, ethical puzzles, downfall, and sacrifice; there is no doubt that Nolan has created a deeply moral film, forcing us to contend with evil in every scene. By the end, though, it doesn't seem that the film has answered its own questions, at least not consistently. From where does evil come? How can we fight it without surrendering to it? Why must one, as more than one character in *The Dark Knight* pronounces, "die a hero or live long enough to see yourself become the villain"?

The film leaves us with a captured villain, a fallen saint, and a Dark Knight—"the hero Gotham deserves, but not the one it needs," as Commissioner Gordon calls

Batman in the film's final lines. The first few times I watched Batman ride off into the fray, taking on the sins of another and living out his noble lie, I felt a tension in my gut: the urge to cheer coupled with an unfinished, haunted feeling. I was suspicious that Nolan had evoked philosophy to give the film a false depth, that he had flung themes and questions at us without the decency to resolve or connect them. Worse, I feared that he might have been manipulating us into applauding for reprehensible, elitist attitudes about truth and human nature by slipping them among chase scenes and explosions.

It didn't seem fair. It is one thing for an art house film to float out questions about evil and let them hang; it is quite another for a summer superhero movie to take the same approach. I could not shake the sense that Nolan was being nebulous where he had every obligation to take a stand.

If Nolan's messages about human nature in *The Dark Knight* seem ambiguous, it is not for lack of reflection on the issue. Evil is at the thematic forefront of every one of his seven films. If we are to make anything of the moral entanglement that emerges in *The Dark Knight*, it makes sense to comb Nolan's catalog for the threads of his worldview. Are there things about human nature he seems to keep saying?

In a 2005 interview with Box Office Mojo, following the release of *Batman Begins*, Nolan addressed the presence of darkness in his films, explaining that "I don't think exclusively in terms of darkness and light—I do think of that, but I also think in terms of what I would call bleakness and richness.... I did feel confident in *Batman Begins* that we had taken material that was in its raw form bleak and given it an emotional resonance that was warmer, if you like."[1] This bleakness/richness dichotomy is perhaps a more cohesive way of characterizing Nolan's worldview than darkness/light or good/evil dichotomies. In the end, it is not that Nolan is inconsistent. I wanted him to tell me a fable because his hero had a cape, but that wasn't fair. Instead, I ought to have applauded him for his commitment to depicting the world as he knows it, the world as it is: grim, complex, pregnant with worth, and never beyond redemption.

Bleakness was Nolan's first language. His first three movies—1998's *Following*, 2000's *Memento*, and 2002's *Insomnia*—seem "simple, miserable, solid all the way through" (to borrow a phrase from *The Prestige*), but they ask resonant questions about human nature and the ease of our descent into evil, questions that Nolan would continue to ask in his later films.

---

1. Nolan, "Wing Kid," interview by Scott Holleran, *Box Office Mojo*, November 20, 2005, http://boxofficemojo.com/features/?id=1921&p=.htm and http://boxofficemojo.com/features/?id=1921&pagenum=2&p=.htm.

In *Following*, Nolan's little-seen first film, the protagonist (Jeremy Theobald) makes a hobby of innocent stalking. His motive is personal curiosity: "You ever . . . just let your eyes rise, go over, drift across a crowd of people, and then slowly start to fix on one person . . . and they've become an individual, just like that." Psychological curiosity becomes a motif of the film when the hero gets taken in by a burglar named Cobb (a precursor to Leonardo DiCaprio's namesake con in *Inception*). Cobb (Alex Haw) may be a thief, but his main thrill comes from stepping inside other people's lives—rifling through their letters, drinking their wine. The characters soon descend past thievery into duplicity, blows, and murder, and inside the neo-noire genre, none of this shocks us. *Following* serves mostly as a training ground for Nolan's kinky structural tastes, but what makes the film interesting is its interest in personhood. As the newly initiated burglar pores over snapshots of his victims, we feel the interplay of anonymity and specificity, a strange "there but for the grace of God go I."

"Everyone has a box," Cobb informs the protagonist. What he means is that all victims have a place to store their secrets, backstories just as lurid as any crime done to them. In one scene, Cobb and his pupil are caught by a returning flat owner, but she seems to turn a blind eye. Cobb explains that she couldn't accuse them because she was sneaking in with a lover. In the gloomy world of *Following*, evil is effortless, and secrets are the tie that binds.

Memento's world is not much brighter. It follows Leonard Shelby (Guy Pearce), who "has this condition": since he was dealt a blow by his wife's rapist and killer, he has been unable to store new memories for longer than a few minutes. Leonard is suspended forever at his moment of deepest pain, his life now driven by the revenge that he has to remind himself to seek. He believes that vengeance will tip the earth further toward justice, even though he will never be able to feel personal vindication. Leonard is haunted by guilt and feels that his fate may be a case of poetic justice. We are asked to root for Leonard's quest for vengeance—his world has been so reduced that it seems it is his only hope to make meaning out of life. But Nolan has said that he believes revenge is "a flaw, a compromise"[2]—perhaps Leonard's is a compromise made with a world too cruel to let him grieve. "John G raped and murdered your wife," the tattoo on Leonard's collarbone reads; his very reality is predicated on an atrocity.

Nolan's next film finds him digging further into the question of human nature and introduces duality as his favorite way to explore it. *Insomnia*, a detective noir picture, follows a more straightforward narrative. Detective Dormer (Al Pacino) is dispatched to Alaska to solve the murder of a high-school girl. In a fog-clouded chase, Dormer accidentally shoots his partner and impulsively lies to cover it up. The only witness to the shooting is the killer he is pursuing, which serves as a curious equalizer.

2. Ibid.

Our hero soon finds himself in a twisted partnership with the villain, united by "how easy it is to kill someone." As the Alaska sun keeps him awake, Dormer loses his grip on reality and his ability to separate himself from the criminal he seeks to capture. In a June 5, 2002, interview with Scott Tobias of the A.V. Club, Nolan talks about his interest in the "moral paradox" of Detective Dormer: "He doesn't have any way, if you think about it, to do the right thing. In fact, it really doesn't matter whether he's doing the right thing." Nolan goes on to describe how audiences become "trapped with" these compromised characters, unable to discern the right course of action any better than the people onscreen, and this is what Nolan believes "noir's all about." Detective Dormer's circumstances, like Leonard Shelby's, are too messy and limited to offer him genuine choice.

The philosophical settings of Nolan's early films are gripping and morally tangled, but as in most crime dramas, they are bleak from the bottom up, with no chance for any kind of enduring redemption. Nolan is concerned with the impulses and paradoxes of human nature, but his characters' paths are restrained by the conventional tragedy and pessimism of film noir. That is, until *Batman Begins*.

Batman—the Caped Crusader, the Dark Knight—is a noir director's dream. But it is clear that Nolan planned to use *Batman Begins* to broaden his message, to take his favorite revenge stories and thicken them with ethics. Bruce Wayne (Christian Bale) has a chip on his shoulder that's just as big as Leonard Shelby's. He watched a mugger kill his parents when he was ten years old, and his hunger for revenge follows him into adulthood. But in *Batman Begins*, revenge is the beginning of the story not the end.

Just as his parents' killer is being released from prison, Bruce has his gun cocked to kill him. As fate would have it, someone beats him to it; he feels robbed. When he tells this to friend and love interest Rachel Dawes,[3] she slaps him and says, "Justice is about harmony. Revenge is about making yourself feel better." Bruce is no less full of rage and regret, but Rachel (the series' idealist) widens his gaze. Bruce realizes that evil is bigger than his own painful past; it's a symptom of a fallen world. He throws his gun to the sea and sets out to find a richer kind of retribution.

Here, Nolan takes the origin story someplace compelling and vital (and, as far as I know, not spelled out in the source material). Bruce abandons his life of privilege to live a poor criminal's life on the other side of the world. He's half looking for a fight and half seeking to understand his enemies. Bruce is desperate and driven, and his heroism is anything but accidental or otherworldly; he is quintessentially *human*. He

---

3. Note that here Dawes is played by Katie Holmes but that in *The Dark Knight* Dawes is played by Maggie Gyllenhaal.

eventually gets taken in by the League of Shadows, an organization that leader Ra's al Ghul (Liam Neeson) assures him shares his hatred of evil and desire for true justice. Bruce then undergoes backbreaking combat training in his quest for "the means to fight injustice; to turn fear against those who prey on the fearful." In Nolan's film, "Batman" is not a superhero but a hard-won vocation; Batman is Bruce's vehicle for his social outrage.

But Bruce soon finds that the League of Shadows seeks a justice that is too brutal. Ra's al Ghul sees evil as a cancer that must be cut off for the sake of the whole; the League of Justice credits itself with the fall of decadent societies throughout history, societies "beyond saving." From his revenge-fueled past, Bruce has come to understand that only compassion can raise justice out of an endless cycle of bloodshed.

Bruce doesn't believe in an eye for an eye, but his mission still requires him to use darkness to fight darkness. The city of Gotham is a bleak place, full of shadowy hideouts. Batman is intended to terrify. He descends on criminals, snarls at them, beats them—but he never kills. Bruce becomes a lout to divert attention from his alter ego. Nolan has loaded up his protagonist with his trademark knotty duality, but this time out, it's different. His first films blurred the lines between hero and villain and let the questions ring. Batman may be dark, but Nolan does not let us forget that he is also a knight. There is a moment, pre-Batman, where Bruce goes down into his cave. Bats descend on him like a plague, the symbols of evil and childhood terror. He collapses in fear but then rises, empowered by the ability to stand inside his nightmare. This scene moves us because it is bleakness made rich. The evils (fear and anger) that pulse inside Bruce push him to fight the evils that lurk outside.

There are two types of evil people in *Batman Begins*: corrupt crooks (like drug lord Falcone, played by Tom Wilkinson) and merciless justice hounds (like Ra's al Ghul). Their common weakness is a reductive view of human nature. Falcone sees people as pathetic and exploitable. Ra's al Ghul sees them as depraved and irredeemable. Both characters see themselves as part of an elite that knows better. Batman's mission is, then, populist: he fights for the sake of humanity at large, fallen Gotham a stand-in for a fallen world.

The question stands, then: *is* Gotham worth saving? And if so, for whose sake? There is a very anti-Nolan moment in the 2002 *Spider-Man* where the citizens of New York City band together to help Spidey antagonize the Green Goblin: "You mess with one of us, you mess with all of us!" Gotham makes no such motion to prove its worth. It's implied that the people of Gotham, in their weakness, have *let* their city become corrupt; they have allowed evil into their world, a kind of original sin. But Nolan never ascribes malevolence to the whole. Gotham is fallen in a more Dostoyevskian sense: people are, in general, weak, and desperation pushes them to evil.

In *The Dark Knight*, the Joker expresses this belief in human depravity: "Their morals, their code... it's a bad joke. Dropped at the first sign of trouble. They're only as good as the world allows them to be. I'll show you. When the chips are down, these civilized people, they'll eat each other." He spends the film bringing chaos to Gotham in an effort to break the city's spirit. In many ways, it seems he succeeds. He claims he'll blow up a hospital if a certain man isn't dead within the hour; citizens make attempts on his life, though Batman sees that he is spared. Batman counts the ferry scene as a victory for human nature, but he doesn't know what really happened in that half hour. And then there is the case of Harvey Dent.

Nolan has described Harvey Dent, Gotham's district attorney and "White Knight," as forming "the emotional arc of the story."[4] For the first half of the film, Harvey serves as a clean counterpart to Batman's vigilante, White Knight to his Dark. He shares Batman's commitment to justice and rounds up criminals with fervor—and despite his wholesomeness, he also shares a bit of Batman's vindictive streak. At one point, he even claims Batman's identity so that he might be arrested in Bruce's place, taking the fall for Bruce's dangerous anonymity. But when the Joker takes away the person he loves most, Harvey's anguish quickly transforms him into an avenger. Like Ra's al Ghul, he now sees justice as balance: a life for a life.

"You thought we could be decent men in an indecent time," barks Harvey in his pain, giving voice to one of Nolan's recurring quandaries. When the chips are down, Harvey—Gotham's symbol of hope—falls into corruption, violence, and finally to his death. As Commissioner Gordon looks down on Harvey's body at the end of the film, he moans, "The Joker won." Batman replies, "The Joker can't win." At first, it seems like denial. But in a moment of morally ambiguous sacrifice, Batman *makes* it true. He places the sins of Harvey, the man, on Batman, the symbol, by claiming Harvey's crimes of revenge as his own. Because of this atonement, the Joker cannot truly succeed in his mission to take down Harvey the hero. While the moment is darkened by Batman's lie and the threat of the dogs sent to hunt him, Nolan ends his film with a grand moral gesture so that we know we are meant to hope.

What Nolan's Gotham gives us is a complex tapestry of human action, a great deal of which is admittedly dishonorable. Indecent times indeed have the tendency to make people indecent. But Nolan has the discernment to give texture to his teeming masses, to explore the insidious nature of groupthink without denying humanity to individuals (as in the upright criminal on the ferry or the impersonators who try to help Batman). We find strains of richness within the film's frantic mobs and intrusions of bleakness in the worthiest of characters. This doesn't mean that Gotham is doomed. Its heroes, though corruptible, are genuinely noble—Bruce Wayne, Harvey

---

4. Nolan, interview by Peter Sciretta, *Slashfilm*, July 17, 2008, http://www.slashfilm.com/interview-christopher-nolan/.

Dent, Rachel Dawes, Commissioner Gordon, Bruce's butler Alfred, his business manager Lucius—despite personal difficulties, each is willing to hope and sacrifice for the sake of the city.

And what of Nolan's other recent films, *The Prestige* and *Inception*? Both are classic Nolan stories, but they represent the opposite poles of his thematic impulses—one revenge, the other redemption. And both are colored by the richer moral possibilities that we see in the Batman films.

Although Nolan has said that he is "not interested in doing a straight revenge story," it seems, at first blush, that *The Prestige* is precisely that.[5] For Nolan's first film after *Batman Begins*, *The Prestige* is a jarring thematic turnaround. It depicts the mutual sabotage of two magicians after their partnership is destroyed by a tragic accident. The event in question is another example of indecent men made from indecent times, and the majority of the film traces the magicians' descent into deception and depravity—a depravity more savage and less ambiguous than anything in Nolan's early films. But it all turns on the linchpin of a final monologue where Hugh Jackman's character explains the reason he has given up his life and his integrity in the pursuit of a magic trick: "The world is simple, miserable, solid all the way through. . . . But if you can fool them even for a second, if you can make them wonder—then you got to see something very special." *The Prestige*'s bleakness emerges from Nolan's sharpened awareness of worldview. The vile tricks of its magicians are their way of making meaning in a materialist world.

Inception, like *Memento*, is concerned with the mysterious sprawl inside the mind and memory, and like *Following* and *Insomnia*, its dream-heist plot sports some questionable ethics. But at its heart is a man hounded by loss and guilt. He lets that guilt chase him into hell and jeopardize the lives of others, but ultimately he chooses the reality of his partners over the tempting fantasy of a dream world. In *The Prestige* deception is the only beauty in a bleak world whereas in *Inception* the hero sacrifices a fabricated love for a fuller reality with his family. Both films show that, post-Batman, Nolan's response to evil has grown out of brainteasers and into a weighty moral maturity.

So, finally: does Nolan believe in a fallen world and in human depravity? It seems that the answer is yes. Bleakness runs through the core of every world he builds. Grief and guilt threaten to tear apart every good thing. But then we consider that only his villains believe in a degenerate humanity. "Never lose your faith in people," Rachel writes to Bruce. The ferries are not destroyed. Alfred continues to help Bruce "pick himself up." Are these optimistic threads mere Hollywood sugarcoating, signs that Nolan is unable to reconcile a superhero's faith with his own dark philosophies?

5. Nolan, "Wing Kid."

For Nolan, the villains are not wrong to believe that people are corruptible. They are wrong to believe that people are past redemption. We have inherited Gotham, a once-great metropolis that we let go to the dogs. Harvey tells us that "you either die a hero or live long enough to see yourself become the villain," and we watch it become his story. In Nolan's Gotham, humans fail. Bruce tries to enact his own human justice with a gun, but it was too small, too bleak. "As a man, I can be weak, I can be ignored," he says. "But as a symbol, I can be incorruptible, I can be everlasting." He needed to become more than a man to give us a justice worthy of the best in humans—and able to withstand the worst.

This, then, is what Rachel means when she tells Bruce to never lose his faith in people. If she had meant merely to trust in people's better nature, she would be a fool. She's a prosecuting attorney in America's dirtiest fictional city. She knows better. Instead, she wants Bruce to hold onto his belief that people matter, that there is some tarnished glory in the human spirit that is worth fighting for. Bruce, the man, has been weak, vengeful, and consumed with fear. He knows better than anyone how miserable men can be, both from the crime done to him and his cowardly response. But he has also seen undeniable honor in his parents, in Rachel, in Commissioner Gordon, in Alfred.

I have a theory that Nolan thinks of himself as something of a Dark Knight. He works in shadows; he sees the world for all its darkness and duality. But he fights to show us the rich, resonating strains of worth that run through our Gotham. *The Dark Knight* enthralled us because Nolan used a comic book flick to speak boldly about our spiritual identity. It shook us because we thought the true tension of human nature that it depicted was too heavy for a popcorn movie. But there we were on the screen: broken, terrified, and nonetheless imbued with a strange majesty.

When *The Dark Knight Rises* premieres, I'll let myself cheer: not for the darkness or ambiguity I'm sure to find but for a director brave enough to show us our world for all its fallenness—and dogged hope.

11 We the Village

by CHAD GUSLER

IN THE DAYS WHEN our courthouse was being built, a mason—we don't know who—came to our village in the night and inscribed a simple phrase on the building's cornerstone: *God's will be done*. We were, at first, outraged that someone had dared to soil our builder's work, but over the course of generations, the mason's phrase became our prayer, our devotion. Even now we gather at the courthouse every morning and evening and say those four words. It's our way of life and God blesses the citizens who heed these words.

And we are blessed. We fish the wide river that flows around us and farm the bottomlands near the banks where the soil is rich. We have four seasons, and our children love them all. Our island is not large, maybe a hundred acres or so, connected to the mainland by a narrow bridge. Not many visit and our lives were quiet until Jonas Tillbottom came our way and tried to ruin us.

Jonas was an unassuming man and we liked him that way, a carpenter and poet, a lover of wood and words. Over the course of the summer, he felt God's call and added his name to the list of men who desired to offer their lives by assuming the role of Village Pastor. Our beloved pastor, Elder Ingold, had died in the early spring, and the time for a new pastor was coming soon. The drawing of a minister was a sacred event, sometimes happening only once in a lifetime, and we were excited to see whom God would choose.

The Sunday of the Lot was humid. The river was low, stranding the skeletal bridge on its pilings above the stinking muck. Little green pools of water bred gnats and mosquitoes, and though they annoyed us, we tolerated them because little creatures have the right to live too. We gathered at the courthouse lawn. Mayor Martin stood on the platform next to his wife, who held seven hymnals, and asked the supplicants to come forward. The men came to the stage, and Mrs. Martin laid the hymnals in a row on a table. We hushed and our children stopped squirming. Each man walked to the table and picked up a hymnal, his hand guided by God. Mayor Martin read Scripture from First Timothy, a passage we knew by heart, about the character of elders and how they must be temperate and have only one wife and not be given over to heavy drink. Some of us say they saw Jonas fidget, shifting his weight from foot to foot, but others say he seemed unmoved, maybe even bored. Mayor Martin prayed and the men opened their hymnals and Jonas drew the Lot, a red strip of paper with a passage from John printed on it. One by one the men filed off the stage until only Jonas and Mayor Martin were left. Then Jonas carefully removed his shirt and Mayor Martin pricked his shoulder with a pin until a little bloody cross was visible to us all. He didn't show the pain, and we all prayed for his faithfulness. "God's will be done," the mayor said.

The iron gates were opened and we proceeded to the cemetery lawn on Church Hill. The willows swayed in the hot breeze, sweeping over the graves, keeping time with the hymns we sang. Jonas's celebration lasted into the evening. We pulled the torches from the church basement and stuck them in the grass. Our children played hide-and-seek among the headstones and markers while we sat contentedly in conversation, our bellies full of cake and punch. The clouds raced across the face of the moon and Jonas sat close to Mary Miller in hushed conversation. We still wonder what words they exchanged.

The following Sunday, Jonas preached his first sermon. It wasn't the best sermon we had ever heard, but it was acceptable. "Love is patient, love is kind," he explained. We know these things—they are dear to our hearts—and it seemed to us an easy topic to preach on, but he was young and just beginning his service. We thought he would get better with time and, indeed, he did improve a little. We watched the summer pass and the river fill with autumn rains. We harvested our corn and turned our gardens under and thanked God for His many gifts.

At first the wet snow was a welcome diversion from the gray of winter. It came down steadily for two days, piling up on trees and roofs. Our children sledded down Church Hill, and Jonas watched their play. He was good with our children, giving them peppermint sticks and caramel chews and hot chocolate, so of course they loved him; in fact, we thought he seemed more comfortable with our children than with us. It didn't take long for word to spread that Mary Miller was with Jonas in his study during those snowy days. The children said that they saw her pale face staring out at the whiteness through the glass.

The air warmed, turning the snow to rain, and the river swelled and rushed under the bridge in a spewing mass and soon overcame our village, toppling our trees and taking our soil. It even heaved a boulder in front of the cemetery, blocking the gate so only the smallest of our children could squeeze through. We thought God to be angry at us, so Jonas held a meeting and prayed to God to stop the rain. It was his first test, but God didn't hear Jonas's prayer: the days were loud, the nights long.

It wasn't until March that we were able to clean up the village. We cut up branches and split fallen trees; we shoveled mud; we tore down some buildings and refurbished others; but the rock remained, so we made a new gate into the cemetery.

Mary Miller suggested that our children decorate the boulder, saying that art could transform it from an eyesore to a story. We agreed, and one Saturday in early April we took our children to the rock. Mary was there with supplies, and they spent the day working. On Sunday, after the service, we admired their work. There were handprints, butterflies, rainbows, and suns. There were portraits of Jesus with children, and there was even a drawing of Jesus raising Lazarus. It was a beautiful rock.

That was the Sunday that Mary began coughing, and she grew worse as the weeks went by, her cough coming from deep within her heaving chest. Some of us thought it was the paint that made her ill, but most believed it was the wet weather. Jonas was downcast much of the spring. His sermons became shorter and he missed meetings. Mayor Martin called the councilmen to a special session. We tried to be understanding, to show him grace, but we the village couldn't be without a pastor for long. He was warned and put on probation.

We thought of sending Mary away. Across the bridge and through the long stretch of forest was an inn for the sick, but she didn't have the strength for the journey, so we called a prayer meeting. Mary Miller lay shriveled on the altar. We cried at the sound of Jonas's weak voice and commiserated with his sorrow. He called for a day of fasting. Our children, who loved Mary most of all, gathered small rocks from the river and painted them, and soon the entrance to her home was stacked knee-high with colorful stones. But prayer didn't help Mary Miller. Doctor Anderson was finally called and, because we knew him as a jovial man, we could tell that Mary's future was bleak when he emerged from her house with a gray face.

"She's very ill," he told us. "I can do nothing."

Mary Miller died in June. Who can stop the will of God? Jonas couldn't do the service, and though we understood his sadness, it was his responsibility. He should have kept his distance from her. We wondered if there was a romance between them, but it was the wrong time to ask. Mayor Martin reluctantly led her funeral service, lauding Mary's strength and faith. "She was the Virtuous Woman," he said, and we all agreed. We buried her three days later and our children gathered around the mound of dirt and sang. Jonas was silent.

Two days after Mary was buried, we saw Jonas, dirty and disheveled, wandering the streets, carrying a shovel. He went to Mary's grave and dug. What drunken mumblings came from inside the gaping hole we do not know—maybe he was possessed by the devil or maybe he conjured a pagan magic—but one thing was clear: when he climbed out of the hole, he had Mary by his side.

He paraded his risen love through the village with childish glee, but all who saw them shut their doors and windows. No shops served him bread and his post wasn't delivered. Who can walk after death? Death is our reminder that no matter what progresses may occur during our short lives, we can't escape Last Breath. Mayor Martin arrested Jonas, and Mary was kept in a cell that we converted from a Sunday school room.

Summer faded and the willows were still. During the day our children played, stopping at dusk when the forest's long shadows stretched across the river and night tried to blacken the stars. October's color was strong, and our river flowed wide. The crops were hardy and the pumpkins turned orange. Things were as they should be.

Justice was swift. Jonas was found guilty of fouling God's will by raising Mary Miller from the dead. That evening we took Jonas to the bridge. Mayor Martin read the verdict and asked Jonas if he had any words. He was silent and didn't look at us. Then Mayor Martin drew the knife and slashed the cross on Jonas's shoulder before sending him away. Banishment is worse than death because when your home is cut from you, you're nobody. Jonas walked across the bridge and didn't once look back.

We tried to keep our children away from Mary, but they flocked around her cell and told her of Jonas's fate. She wailed and the owls answered her screeches and our children were frightened. We had to decide what to do with her. Some said that they didn't like her locked up in the church basement because they could hear her voice rising through the furnace grates when we sang our hymns on Sunday mornings. Others said she smelled of death, including the janitor, who said that no amount of lemon balm could rid the building of her stench. In late November the councilmen met for nearly a week and deliberated Mary's fate. Mayor Martin announced the decision.

"We have to undo what Jonas did so we can return to God His will," he said.

December was cold. We led Mary to her painted boulder by the old cemetery gate. The machinist, a large, blind man who never spoke, drilled a hole into the rock and fastened an iron ring into it. He shackled Mary to the rock. She did not cry, nor did she refuse our children who touched her until we had them sent home. We gave her water to drink.

On Christmas Eve, a cold wind rushed down the river and bore through our village. Mary died the next day and we felt lightened, as if our breath could again move freely through our lungs. The machinist loosened her chains and we watched him stumble along with her frozen body. He took her to the river and with a great heave, he pushed her across the ice and she broke through, slipping into the black water, returning to God His will.

12 Randomness and Assurance: Does Everything Happen for a Reason?

by GREGORY A. BOYD

THE BLUEPRINT WORLDVIEW

On August 1, 2007, a highway bridge several miles from my house collapsed during rush hour, killing 13 people and wounding 144 others. That night, a well-known local pastor blogged about a discussion he had with his eleven-year-old daughter as he put her to bed. He asked her what purpose God might have had for not "holding up that bridge," even though he could have done so with "his pinky." He affirmed her when she responded that God "wanted all the people of Minneapolis to fear him."[1]

The assumption behind this young lady's answer is that everything happens for a reason—it's all part of a grand divine plan. This assumption has dominated Christian theology since Augustine in the fifth century, and I have elsewhere labeled it the "blueprint worldview" because it holds that every detail in history happens in strict accordance with an eternal blueprint that resides in the mind of God.[2] The blueprint worldview is expressed in some of the most famous hymns of the church, such as William Cowper's famous eighteenth-century piece, "God Moves in a Mysterious Way." This hymn encourages believers to "judge not the Lord by feeble sense, / but trust Him for His grace," for "behind a frowning providence, / He hides a smiling face." Whatever the nightmare that you or a loved one may be going through, we are

---

1. John Piper, "Putting My Daughter to Bed Two Hours after the Bridge Collapsed," *desiringGod*, August 1, 2007, http://www.desiringgod.org/blog/posts/putting-my-daughter-to-bed-two-hours-after-the-bridge-collapsed.
2. Boyd, *God at War: The Bible and Spiritual Conflict* (Downers Grove, IL: InterVarsity, 1997), ch. 1.

encouraged to accept that God ordained it for a good reason, which, presumably, is why he is "smiling" as it unfolds.[3]

So far as I can tell, this view is about as prevalent today as it ever was. It's reflected in the many clichés Christians, as well as non-Christians, often mutter in the face of tragedies: "Everything happens for a reason," "God has his reasons," "God's ways are not our ways," "Providence writes straight with crooked lines," "Nothing happens by accident," "God knows what he is doing," "God's timing is the right timing," and so on. Although the blueprint worldview reflected in these clichés produces rage toward God in the hearts of some sufferers, it provides a great deal of comfort to those believers who feel assured that, however terrible their suffering or the suffering of a loved one may be, at least that suffering is neither without purpose nor permanent. It is all part of God's grand plan.

To understand the traditional theology supporting this perspective, it's helpful to distinguish between a *strong* and a *weak* version of the blueprint worldview. The strong version is usually associated with Calvinism, a school of thought which believes that God eternally predetermines all that comes to pass. In this view, everything happens for a reason because God *wills* everything to unfold exactly as it does. The weak version is usually associated with Arminianism, a school of thought which believes that God created people and angels with free will, though God eternally foreknows what they will do. In this view, everything happens for a reason because God *allows* everything to unfold exactly as it does.[4]

Although there are obviously significant differences between these two versions of the blueprint worldview, both are grounded in the same, apparently straightforward, line of reasoning: if God is omnipotent, as all orthodox Christians believe, he has the power to do *whatever he wants*. He therefore possesses the ability to bring about anything he wants or at least to prevent anything from happening *if he wants to*. From this it seems to follow that everything that happens does so because God wanted it to happen, or at least because God did not want to prevent it from happening. And if God is perfectly good and perfectly wise, as all orthodox Christians believe, it also seems to follow that God has a perfectly good and wise reason for why he chose to bring about every specific thing that happens or at least for why he chose not to prevent every specific thing that happens. And so, whether God specifically willed it or specifically allowed it, everything happens for a reason.

---

3. Cowper, "God Moves in a Mysterious Way," http://www.cyberhymnal.org/htm/g/m/gmovesmw.htm.

4. Although people who believe that everything is predetermined obviously advocate the strong version of the blueprint worldview, not everyone who believes that God foreknows how humans and angels will behave is an advocate of the weak version of this blueprint. Some contemporary Arminians espouse what is often called "simple foreknowledge," which is the view that although God eternally foreknows all that will come to pass, he does not possess the ability to do anything to alter it.

I believe both the strong and weak versions of the blueprint worldview are misguided. In this essay, however, I will focus only on the weak version. I do this because I believe that whatever valid objections I raise against the weak version will apply *a fortiori* to the strong version, whereas the converse is not true. I will first review the blueprint worldview's approach to the problem of evil and then address several challenges this worldview faces in the light of Scripture. I will then argue that the apparently straightforward line of reasoning that leads to the blueprint worldview is in fact misguided. As counterintuitive as it may initially sound, I will argue that affirming the omnipotence of God does *not* entail that God can prevent any event he wants to. I will thus argue that believing in God's omnipotence does not mean we must accept that everything that happens, including fatal bridge collapses, does so for a reason. Yet, I will close by contending that this does not mean suffering is gratuitous. So long as we remain confident in God's infinite intelligence, I will argue, we can embrace the same assurance the blueprint worldview offers without denying the randomness of evil events.

THE PROBLEM OF EVIL

There's no denying that one can find support in Scripture for the blueprint worldview. For example, Luke tells us that although Jesus's crucifixion was done "with the help of wicked men," it nevertheless took place "by God's deliberate plan and foreknowledge" (Acts 2:23 TNIV). Clearly, the freely chosen actions of those who crucified Jesus fit into a grand divine plan. Similarly, the author of Hebrews encourages believers facing persecution to "endure hardship as discipline" from God (Heb. 12:7). It's again clear that the freely chosen actions of those who persecuted these early Christians serve a divine purpose. And although Joseph's brothers mistreated Joseph of their own free will, he later told them that although their intent was to harm him, "God intended it for good" (Gen. 50:20). These kinds of passages make it impossible for anyone who takes Scripture seriously to deny that there is at least some truth to the blueprint worldview.

But does this perspective tell the whole story? There are both philosophical and biblical reasons to think not. The main philosophical challenge to the weak version of the blueprint worldview concerns the problem of evil.[5] Although there is little difficulty accepting that God may *sometimes* have a specific reason for allowing a particular evil event to take place, it is challenging to accept that this is the case for

---

5. The *strong* version of the blueprint worldview faces other philosophical challenges, such as the question of how humans and angels can be held morally responsible for engaging in evil acts that God predestines them to commit while, conversely, God is held to be all holy (and not morally responsible) for predestining them to do so.

each and every evil event. Some events manifest a depth of evil for which it seems almost obscene to suppose they happened for a divine reason.

For example, in my book *God at War*, I discuss an eyewitness account of a six-year-old Jewish girl named Zosia whose beautiful eyes were plucked out by the bare hands of two Nazi guards in front of her horrified mother.[6] The mother went insane and both were subsequently gassed in one of Adolf Hitler's concentration camps. It makes some sense to me to affirm that this event happened "for a reason" if by this one is assuming there was something that motivated *the guards* to choose to carry out this atrocity. But it's challenging, to say the least, to affirm that this event happened "for a reason" if by this one is assuming there was a specific, perfectly good and perfectly wise reason that motivated *God* to choose to *not* prevent this specific atrocity. If we allow ourselves to vividly imagine this terrorized little girl pinned to the ground while getting her eyes plucked out, does it not become obscene to suppose that this is brought about by a "frowning providence" that hides God's "smiling face"?

Consider that if God deemed it *better* to allow this nightmare than to prevent it, we must also believe that it would have been *bad* had Zosia's torture been prevented. We must thus accept that God's perfectly wise and perfectly good plan for the universe would have been *less* good and *less* wise if Zosia and her mother had been spared. And this we must accept for every single child and adult who were tortured and gassed under Hitler's demonic regime as well as for every unthinkable nightmare people have experienced throughout history. God's grand plan would have been somehow *tarnished*, we must believe, had one less child been kidnapped, raped, and mutilated or had one less person been tortured by the corrupted church in the Middle Ages and by demented world leaders such as Josef Stalin, Pol Pot, and Idi Amin.

I fully accept Cowper's encouragement to refrain from judging God's ways "by feeble sense" and to instead "trust Him for His grace." Believers must expect to encounter a great deal of mystery as we ponder the ways of God. But at least for me, to affirm that God specifically allows evil events such as these as part of his greater plan is to move from legitimate mystery into sheer incoherence.

PROBLEMS WITH SCRIPTURE

Although Scripture contains many examples of God allowing evil for specific reasons, it also contains many examples in which God must engage in conflict with rebellious opposing spiritual forces. In fact, I've elsewhere argued that God's conflict with opposing spiritual forces forms one of the central motifs of the biblical narrative.[7] In

---

6. Boyd, *God at War*, 33–36.
7. See Boyd, *God at War*.

the Old Testament, these forces are rebellious subordinate gods, hostile waters, and cosmic monsters (e.g., the Leviathan) that all ancient Near Eastern people believed surrounded and perpetually threatened the earth. In the New Testament, the opposing spiritual forces God must battle are Satan, principalities and powers, and demons.

There are biblical grounds for believing that the infinitely wise God always finds a way to use the evil he battles to further his sovereign purposes, but nowhere in this central biblical motif do we find the slightest hint that *the battle itself* was allowed, let alone willed, for a specific higher purpose. Indeed, the very fact that God must engage in genuine conflict with opposing forces and rely on his wisdom to overcome them suggests to me that he *can't* simply use his omnipotent power to prevent their evil activity. I will address the paradox of how there can be things an omnipotent God can't do in a moment, but first we must consider other biblical material that conflicts with the blueprint worldview.

Given that Jesus is the one and only perfect revelation of God (e.g., Heb. 1:3), our understanding of God's conflict with opposing forces should be based primarily on his ministry. Jesus spent his entire ministry among people who in one way or another were suffering. Yet he *never once* suggested that their suffering was for a reason. Never do we find any suggestion that people's afflictions somehow fit into a grand divine plan. To the contrary, Jesus and the Gospel authors uniformly diagnosed people's afflictions as being due to the work of Satan and/or demons (e.g., Mark 9:25 and Luke 11:14 and 13:11–16).[8] And far from suggesting that people's afflictions had anything to do with God's will, Jesus manifested the will of God by *freeing* people from their demonically influenced infirmities.

Peter would later summarize Jesus's entire ministry to Cornelius by proclaiming that Jesus "went around doing good and healing all who were under the power of the devil" (Acts 10:38). In doing this, we are elsewhere taught that Jesus destroyed "the works of the devil" (1 John 3:8) and broke "the power of him who holds the power of death—that is, the devil" (Heb. 2:14). Such teachings should lead us to conclude that if infirmities happen for a reason, the reason is found in Satan and other forces of evil that oppose God. The only reason for afflictions that has anything to do with God is for people to be set free from them and for the forces that oppress people to be overthrown.

As a matter of fact, Jesus several times explicitly *rebuked* the suggestion that tragedies happened for a reason. For example, when certain people speculated, in good blueprint fashion, that Pilate's massacre of a group of Galileans served a divine purpose, Jesus responded by asking them, "Do you think that these Galileans were worse sinners than all the other Galileans because they suffered this way? I tell you,

---

8. For a complete discussion of Jesus' healing and deliverance ministry and how it undermines the blueprint worldview, see Boyd, *God at War*, ch. 6.

no!" Whatever purpose led to the massacre of those unfortunate people resided in Pilate, *not* God (Luke 13:1–3).

Along the same lines, in response to this crowd's blueprint belief that God was somehow behind a natural disaster involving a tower that collapsed and killed eighteen people in Siloam, Jesus asked, "Do you think they were more guilty than all the others living in Jerusalem? I tell you no!" Instead of getting involved in misguided speculations about what purpose God had for allowing people to perish, Jesus instructed these people to focus on turning their own lives around, lest they perish (Luke 13:4–5). If someone wants to discern the reason natural disasters occur, the fact that Jesus responded to a life-threatening storm by rebuking it, just as he did demons, should not lead them to God but to the spiritual forces that oppose God and that corrupt nature (Mark 4:37–39).[9]

Finally, just as there is no suggestion in Scripture that there is a divine purpose behind God's conflict with spiritual opponents, so too we find no hint of a divine purpose behind God's conflict with rebellious humans. Beginning with Adam and Eve in the Garden of Eden and continuing throughout the biblical narrative, we find God giving people the choice to follow him or not. And when they choose to rebel, it is almost uniformly understood to reflect *their* own purposes and to stand in *opposition to* God's purposes.[10] So, for example, Luke notes that "the Pharisees and the experts in the law *rejected God's purpose for themselves*" by rejecting John's baptism (Luke 7:30, emphasis added). And in Isaiah, Yahweh rebukes his "obstinate children" who "carry out plans that are *not* mine, forming an alliance, but *not* by my Spirit, heaping sin upon sin" (Isa. 30:1, emphasis added). Far from being allowed for a specific sovereign purpose, we see that sin is sin precisely because it *conflicts* with God's sovereign purpose. In this light, I would again submit that if someone wants to look for a reason behind Zosia's torture, they should look for it in the guards who tortured her, not in God.

---

9. To read more about Jesus treating this storm like a demon, see Boyd, *God at War*, 211. This is not to suggest that there is a specific demonic being behind every particular natural disaster but that were it not for the corrupting influence of demonic beings, nature would not afflict us the way it sometimes does. See Boyd, "Evolution as Cosmic Conflict," in *Creation Made Free: Science and Open Theology*, ed. J. Oord (Eugene, OR: Wipf and Stock, 2009), 125–45. See also S. Webb, *The Dome of Eden: A New Solution to the Problem of Creation and Evolution* (Eugene, OR: Cascade Books, 2010), 147–52. I should note that many see John 9:1–3 as an example of Jesus affirming that God was involved in a man being born blind. Even if this is granted, it is the one exception to the otherwise uniform perspective of the Gospels and cannot be legitimately used to overturn this perspective. But I have elsewhere argued that this passage actually provides another example of Jesus rebuking people for speculating about God's supposed role in people's afflictions (*God at War*, 231–36).

10. I say "almost uniformly" to account for those several instances in which Yahweh is said to "harden" someone's heart, such as he did with Pharaoh (e.g., Exod. 9:12 and 10:20). Even here, however, I argue that Yahweh's hardening is a disciplinary action taken in *response* to human sin, which originated in people's own will, not God's. It's significant, for example, that Scripture says Pharaoh hardened his own heart *before* it says God hardened it (e.g., Exod. 8:15 and 8:32).

THE LOGIC OF FREE WILL

With very few exceptions, Christian thinkers throughout church history have agreed that there are certain things an omnipotent God can't do, such as create a married bachelor, a round triangle, or a rock so heavy he can't lift it. The reason God can't do these things is because they are not really *things* at all. They are, rather, self-contradictions and are therefore devoid of meaning. A bachelor is by definition not married. A triangle is by definition not round. And rocks, by definition, have a finite weight and can always be lifted up by an omnipotent God. The problem with the blueprint worldview is that it fails to apply this logic to the concept of free will.

There are, of course, an almost endless number of highly complex and hotly contested philosophical issues surrounding the concept and conditions of free will, but for our purposes here I submit a brief, less nuanced definition: agents are free if and only if they have the capacity to resolve, by their own power, two or more *possible* courses of action into one *actual* course of action.[11] Free will, in short, is our self-determining capacity to choose to go *this* way or *that* way. It's my conviction that God created us with this capacity because his ultimate goal for creation, so far as it is revealed to us, includes humans entering into an eternal love relationship with him and with one another. Yet, as Tatian and other early church fathers so clearly understood, it is logically impossible for contingent beings such as ourselves to enter into a genuinely loving and morally significant relationship with God or with other people unless we have the capacity to choose for or against it.[12]

Of course, God certainly could have created us in such a way that we would *have* to always perform loving actions, speak loving words, think loving thoughts, and even experience loving feelings. But unless we possess the self-determining capacity to choose *against* these things, God would know, even if we did not, that our decision to engage in these things was not *our* decision at all; it was, rather, *his* decision when he predetermined us to engage in these things. I would argue along the same lines for angelic beings: the very fact that some angels rebelled against God and are destined to be punished for this implies that they were created with something analogous to our morally significant capacity to say yes or no to God's love.

If this understanding of free will is accepted, we can begin to see why God cannot prevent certain events, despite the fact that he is all-powerful and despite the fact that he would like to do so. Suppose God has endowed someone we'll call Charlie with the self-determining capacity to go this way or that way—*this* way representing a way that God approves of and *that* way representing a way God disapproves of.

---

11. I have explored these matters in detail in Boyd, *Satan and the Problem of Evil: Constructing a Trinitarian Warfare Theodicy* (Downers Grove, IL: InterVarsity, 2001), especially ch. 2–6.

12. Tatian, *Address to the Greeks*, 7, in *The Ante-Nicene Fathers*, eds. A. Roberts and J. Donaldson, vol. 2 (Grand Rapids, MI: Eerdmans, 1979), 67.

If God prevents Charlie from going *that* way because he disapproves of it, then he clearly didn't endow Charlie with the self-determining capacity to go this way or that way. For God to endow Charlie with free will, we see, means that, by definition, God cannot coercively prevent Charlie from going that way simply because he doesn't approve of it. Charlie's free will must, by definition, be irrevocable. The concept of God preventing Charlie from going that way, though he's endowed him with the capacity to go this way or that way, is as self-contradictory as the concept of a married bachelor, a round triangle, or a rock so heavy God can't lift it.

Of course, the free will that God endowed Charlie with is limited in scope and duration, as is the case with the free will of every created being. Therefore, there are limits to how much and how long God must tolerate Charlie making decisions he disapproves of, as is also true for every created free agent. And Scripture assures us there will come a time when every created agent's capacity to "go that way" will be used up and when the entire creation will therefore be free of evil. Until that time, however, the extent to which God has endowed agents with the capacity to resolve, of their own power, two or more possible courses of action into one actual course of action must be the extent to which God, by definition, cannot unilaterally prevent events from happening just because he doesn't approve of them.[13]

To my way of thinking, this perspective on free will explains why God, though he is all-powerful, engages in genuine conflict with opposing spiritual forces and opposing humans. It also explains why Scripture celebrates God's *wisdom*, and not just his power, in governing the world, engaging in battle, and bringing good out of evil (e.g., 1 Cor. 1:30 and 2:7; Rom. 7:12 and 16:27). One only needs wisdom when one has to outsmart an opponent or solve problems, things that God would never need to do if he could simply coercively prevent anything from happening that he didn't approve of. And this perspective makes sense in explaining why the God of the Bible is often portrayed as getting exasperated and grieved when he tries unsuccessfully to get obstinate people to align themselves with his will (e.g., Jer. 3:6–7 and 19-20, Ezek. 22:30–31, and Isa. 63:10). The God we find in Scripture is sovereign without being microcontrolling, and in my opinion, his sovereignty is all the more praiseworthy for this reason.[14]

---

13. This is not to suggest that God can't *influence* free agents to go this way and not go that way, so long as this influence stops short of taking away these agents' God-given capacity to go this way or that way.

14. For a more comprehensive and detailed fleshing out of issues surrounding this perspective, see Boyd, *Satan and the Problem of Evil* as well as Boyd, *Is God to Blame? Beyond Pat Answers to the Problem of Suffering* (Downers Grove, IL: InterVarsity, 2003).

ACCEPTING RANDOMNESS WITH ASSURANCE

If we accept that God's goal for humans is centered on love and that this love requires a free choice, and if we accept that this free choice is, by definition, irrevocable for a significant length of time, then the only "reason" for events that are the result of free decisions is found in the agents themselves, not in God. We thus need not speculate about a divine reason for Zosia's atrocity or any other atrocity. Moreover, if we accept the biblical witness regarding the existence and authority of good and evil angelic beings, we can say the same thing about natural evil. As the early church fathers uniformly understood, whether we're talking about physical infirmities or injurious earthquakes, we may presume that all suffering that occurs from natural causes is ultimately due to the fallen state of creation and to the cosmic rebellion of angelic free agents who use their God-given authority over aspects of creation at cross-purposes with God.[15] Hence, we may affirm that *everything* in creation that is inconsistent with the character of God, as revealed in Christ, is ultimately due to wills other than God's.

I have no doubt that some readers will find this perspective disturbing, however, for it means we must accept the apparent randomness of evil at face value. There is, in this view, no higher reason to explain why Zosia had her eyes plucked out while other girls in her vicinity were spared. This randomness grows even more disturbing if we consider the many free decisions that factored into Zosia's atrocity. For example, for all we know, there were a thousand free decisions Zosia's mother made in the days, weeks, and months preceding the moment of the attack that, had any one been different, may have prevented her and her daughter from being precisely where they were when the Nazi guards noticed Zosia's beautiful eyes. The same can be said about an innumerable number of other people whose decisions exercised, or could have exercised, any degree of influence on this unfortunate woman and her daughter. The same holds true for the two guards as well as for Hitler—for all we know, had any one of an unfathomable number of free decisions that exercised any degree of influence on Hitler, his colleagues, his enemies, his parents, or his grandparents been different, he may not have become the führer of the Third Reich. He may not have attempted to annihilate the Jewish people and Zosia may have consequently been spared.

In this light, we can only conclude that these kinds of tragedies are the result of an unfathomable number of random events. And we have not even considered the unknowable, but nevertheless real, free decisions of the myriad of angelic agents who undoubtedly exercised some degree of influence in bringing Zosia's tragic episode about. Looking into this vast abyss of arbitrariness can indeed be disturbing, for it

---

15. See Boyd, *Satan and Problem of Evil*, ch. 8–10. This is in no way to deny that humans frequently share responsibility for so-called natural evils that afflict us, given that it is becoming abundantly clear that our free decisions affect our environment, for better or for worse, in a much more profound way than previous generations ever imagined.

seems to suggest that Zosia's suffering, and all such suffering, is devoid of meaning. This is undoubtedly one of the reasons the blueprint worldview is attractive to many people despite its formidable problems. If the blueprint worldview is true—if everything happens for a reason—then we can rest assured that Zosia's suffering, and all suffering, occurs for a good and wise purpose. Evil and suffering are not random and do not have the last word.

The longing for suffering to have a purpose is both understandable and legitimate. But if we remain confident that God is all knowing and infinitely wise, I don't believe the blueprint worldview is our only means of having such peace. For although the innumerable free decisions that factored into Zosia's suffering constitute an unfathomable abyss to us, they surely do not to God. To the contrary, if God is all-knowing and infinitely intelligent, he foresaw from all eternity the possibility that every one of the innumerable free decisions that factored into Zosia's torture might occur just as they did. Not only this, he must have foreseen every other possible way these free decisions might have gone. Indeed, he must have foreseen from eternity each and every possible decision that each and every possible free agent could ever make and how all these possible decisions could possibly interact with each other. And because his intelligence has no limits, God must have anticipated each and every one of these innumerable possibilities as though it was the only possibility he had to consider.

Some theologians have claimed that unless God foreknows the future as a domain of settled facts, he cannot guarantee that his plan will bring good out of evil.[16] Although they don't intend it, this claim actually insults God's intelligence, for only a God of limited intelligence would be better prepared for one certain future as opposed to a myriad of possible ones. If we remain confident in God's infinite intelligence, we can rest assured that God has an eternally prepared plan on how to bring good out of evil for each and every possible tragedy that could ever possibly come to pass. And we can be confident that this plan is as perfect as it would have been had the tragedy been specifically allowed by him for the very purpose of the good he plans to bring out of it, in case it occurs. We thus need not believe that evil events happen *for* a perfectly good and wise purpose in order to believe that evil events happen *with* a perfectly good and wise purpose. That is, specific tragedies don't happen *because* they fit into an eternal divine plan, but God nevertheless has an eternally prepared plan *for* every specific tragedy that might ever possibly come to pass.

---

16. See for example, Bruce A. Ware, *God's Lesser Glory: The Diminished God of Open Theism* (Wheaton, IL: Crossway Books, 2000); and John M. Frame, *No Other God: A Response to Open Theism* (Phillipsburg, NJ: P&R, 2001). For fuller responses to this frequent claim, see Boyd, "Neo-Molinism and the Infinite Intelligence of God," *Philosophia Christi* 5.1 (2003): 187–204; and "The Open Theism View," in *Divine Foreknowledge: Four Views*, eds. James K. Beilby and Paul R. Eddy (Downers Grove, IL: InterVarsity, 2001), 13–47.

Thus, we do not need to accept that Zosia's nightmare was part of a "frowning providence" concealing God's "smiling face" and that God planned her torture for some greater purpose. I, for one, believe God wept as this arbitrary demonstration of demonic evil was being carried out. Yet I also believe that God, from before the creation of the world, had been preparing a contingency plan to redeem good out of this atrocity, just in case it tragically came to pass.

13 Thoughts on African American Theology and Suffering as Moral Evil

by ANTHONY B. PINN

For several centuries African American Christianity, in the form of black churches and the theological language of those churches, has worked to silence the moans and groans of African Americans experiencing racial, gender, and class-based oppression. This oppression gives shape to what many academics call moral evil, that is, human-generated destruction of life based on patterns of targeted discrimination and dehumanization as opposed to natural disasters such as earthquakes.

Although certain dilemmas resulting from the experience of moral evil are easily addressed and handled with little energy and few complaints, moral evil as experienced by African Americans has not been so easy to manage. As philosopher of religion William R. Jones noted almost four decades ago, moral evil's impact on African Americans is disproportionate and unto death.[1] In significant ways, the perception of black churches as centers of existential and ontological meaning hinges on their ability to provide compelling answers to the question of moral evil. Unfortunately, the typical response of these churches to moral evil has entailed some form of compromise with suffering.

African American Christians sitting in black churches have been encouraged to address moral evil through the framework of theodicy and the language of redemptive suffering. Put differently, they have been conditioned to ask a numbing question: what can be said about God in light of human suffering in the world? If they answer that suffering is a means by which God's will is achieved, they have reduced the significance of their physical confrontation with the world, favoring instead promises of

---

1. See Jones, *Is God a White Racist? A Preamble to Black Theology* (1973; Boston, MA: Beacon, 1996).

heaven and/or historical liberation that is somewhat disembodied. At best, such an approach is a labyrinth so full of twists and turns that those moving through it forget for the moment their angst. At worst, it encourages African Americans to sanction and participate in their own demise. Within the context of African American Christian doctrine and theology, some combination of these two outcomes is too often the case.

JUST A BIT OF CONTEXT

Beginning with the spirituals, African American Christians have demonstrated a perspective on suffering that is marked by an epistemological tension between their embodied suffering and the transhistorical marker of suffering as a divine activity exemplified through the Christ event. This idea of suffering as a divine activity is based on an assumption that the suffering of Jesus the Christ and the suffering of African Americans are mediated through proper relationship to God. In this way, suffering serves as a litmus test of sorts, a means by which one's spiritual health is verified. As so many African Americans proclaim, "no cross, no crown." Moreover, as others note (without concern for the irony, or at least the signification involved), God does not give us more than we can bear. Yet at what point does death dealing and disproportionate oppression become too much to bear? At the point of uncontrolled, inexplicable pain? At the loss of all that matters existentially? Or at the loss of ontological certainty, that is, at the point of death?

Many people who consider the relationship between God and suffering believe that because God is loving, kind, and just, all suffering must have a purpose toward compassionate ends; it must be productive. Others explain the discomfort and shortcomings of life as part of a larger cosmic scheme that pits God against Satan, a demonic force which either serves as an ontological reality or a counter symbol: "But if you haven't the good Lord in your heart / The Devil will get you sure."[2] According to this theological reading, God ultimately uses even the damage done in human history by that figure for a positive outcome, but this "positive" outcome does not demand the safeguarding of embodied existence.

African American cultural production of a Christian orientation is ripe with this perspective, and such theological thinking is also prevalent within the public conversations and private reflections of African American "church folk." Committed Christian Phillis Wheatley's poetry speaks to the liberating nature of the African suffering that resulted from the slave trade by suggesting that the harsh movement across the Atlantic brought Africans in contact with the Christian faith: "Remember,

---

2. William Stickles, "Hard Trials," http://www.negrospirituals.com/news-song/hard_trials.htm.

Christians, Negros, black as Cain, / May be refin'd and join th'angelic train."[3] Early church leaders spoke a similar word in that, despite moments of doubt, they typically recognized the pedagogical importance of suffering. They understood that moral evil is not ideal and that it is not part of God's perfect will, yet they also believed that moral evil does not bring into question God's will. Even in the context of misery, God's positive plan for African Americans can be fulfilled. This line of theological reasoning is evident in the writings and speeches of even the most radical of church figures, such as Henry McNeal Turner who promoted an understanding of African American suffering as a prime source of refinement and progress ordained and monitored by God.[4]

Moving from the period of slavery to the Jim Crow restrictions, the Christian dimension of the civil rights movement was held hostage by this perception of suffering as an inevitable presence and an ethical virtue. A clear mantra could be heard from various pulpits and platforms that unmerited suffering is redemptive. But again, how does one assess and differentiate merited suffering from its unmerited counterpart? What is the appropriate hermeneutic for establishing this differentiation?

IS THE ANSWER IN THE LYNCHING TREE?

This economy of moral evil has dominated church thought and has shaped African American Christian practice—all supported by African American theologians. Taking their cue from the theological structures of meaning and expression offered by the spirituals and the sensibilities of a range of religious leaders, African American theologians have worked to maintain a liberating balance between the deadly nature of moral evil and the assumed truth of the Christ event as God's yes to fulfilled life.

The most widely quoted and celebrated of these theologians is James Cone. In his most recent work, he wrestles with the theological nature and meaning of moral evil through an impassioned discussion of how the cross and the lynching tree serve as the nexus of both tragedy and triumph.[5] Beyond summing up some of the more significant of his theological points made over the course of forty some years, Cone provides a cartography of suffering as an endemic dimension of salvation history with great bearing on how Christians should construct their ethical existence. The cross and the lynching tree, he argues, are existential and ontological markers of the

---

3. Wheatley, "On Being Brought from Africa to America," http://www.vcu.edu/engweb/webtexts/Wheatley/phil.htm.

4. See Turner, *Respect Black: The Writings and Speeches of Henry McNeal Turner*, ed. Pinn (New York, NY: Arno, 1968); and *Making the Gospel Plain: The Writings of Bishop Reverdy C. Ransom*, ed. Pinn (Harrisburg, PA: Trinity Press International, 1999).

5. Cone, *The Cross and the Lynching Tree* (Maryknoll, NY: Orbis Books, 2011).

substance of Christian faith and the demands made on that faith in the face of ongoing injustice.

Although compelling in certain respects, the underbelly of Cone's argument is its failure to fully grasp the blood and guts of humanity's religious confrontation with the absurdity of life. Cone and other theologians like him tend to sidestep the more robust challenges to the radical Christology offered in the tradition of African American theology. For instance, Jones raises questions concerning the guts or substance of christological claims by questioning the reading of historical evidence offered by African American theologians such as Cone. The historical record, Jones suggests, can be read in such a way as to make the suffering of African Americans a part of God's plan for the world—if one takes seriously what appears to be the success of Caucasian Americans as a group over African Americans. In addition, even if the Christ event is granted, Jones wonders what it can mean for African American suffering given that it takes place prior to the enslavement of African Americans and that it is part of a larger narrative which fails to challenge the structural importance of enslavement.[6]

Cone's initial response to this critique in 1975 involved the rehearsal of the Christ event's centrality to African American thought and life. According to Cone, Jones's failure to recognize this centrality meant that his challenge was a matter of external critique, and this type of challenge did not merit full attention and consideration. However, Cone now responds to this ongoing critique in a way meant to historically ground Christology in the demands of African American life. That is to say, Cone suggests that the lynching tree makes immediately real and tangible the truth of the cross.[7] For Cone, such a theological move fosters a thick connection between the existential circumstances of black life and the transcendent principles of divine sympathy noted through the cross. The cross is made contemporary, a challenge in real time. This synergy pushes beyond even the best of the liberal theological tradition by remaining focused on the stench of oppression as the sensual arena for Christian engagement. For Cone, liberal theology is distant in that it is a secondhand discourse much too safe from the consequences of life. "It," writes Cone, "is one thing to teach theology (like Niebuhr, Barth, Tillich, and most theologians) in the safe environs of

---

6. Jones, *Is God a White Racist?*

7. Cone provides an initial response to Jones in *God of the Oppressed* (New York, NY: Harper and Row, 1975), ch. 8. Cone not only objected to the framing of black suffering as a philosophical issue—an issue he assumed lacked urgency and required a certain luxury of thought not afforded African Americans due to their suffering. Cone was also concerned with the normative status of the Christ event and the metanarrative of salvation history as proper responses to black suffering in any historical context. My extension of African American nontheistic humanist theology has met with a similar response from Cone and those holding to his basic position. See, for example, Dwight Hopkins, review of *Why, Lord? Suffering and Evil in Black Theology*, by Pinn, *African American Review* 31.3 (Fall 1997); and Sherman Jackson, *Islam and Black Suffering* (New York, NY: Oxford University Press, 2009).

a classroom and quite another to live one's theology in a situation that entails the risk of one's life." The pressing reality of the cross and the lynching tree force the presence of death in one's commitment to life.[8]

One might think this christological posturing would be less compelling when the critique is offered as an internal critique—that is, a critique advanced by someone who claims the Christian faith—yet Cone's response to Delores Williams's brilliant challenge to traditional atonement theory meets with quick rejection. Williams argues that the shedding of blood associated with the Christ event does not speak to a liberating moment. It is nothing to model in that it points to human failure—the inability of humans to embrace a transformative moment. Williams wants to reject any sense of blood as redemptive and instead sees the Christ event as an ethical prompt—a contemplative moment during which to reflect on how we ought to behave in the world and how we ought to be in relationship with self/others. From Williams's perspective, fixation on a bloody cross promotes a surrogate posture that is damning to African Americans in general and African American women in particular. This challenge, unlike that offered by Jones, does not require a rejection of theistic responses to human suffering; rather, she proposes greater attention to practice, to the ministry of Christ as an exemplar of conduct. Hence, it is not the shedding of blood—whether on the cross or the lynching tree—that is of paramount importance.[9]

Cone recognizes this challenge but does not find it compelling. Through his appeal to the Christ event, Cone links the cross and the lynching tree as signs of death and life. They are tropes shrouded in mystery in that "instead of attempting to explain the saving power of the cross rationally, black Christians recognized it as a mystery, beyond human understanding or control." If some African Americans experience the cross as something that "sustained them—not for suffering but in their resistance to it," removed is any need to unpack the nature of moral evil. Or, in other words, "the cross is the burden we must bear in order to attain freedom."[10]

Cone tends to argue that redemptive suffering arguments don't exist if there is an effort to end suffering; that is to say, redemptive suffering arguments, according to Cone, involve a level of passivity that isn't present in most African American religious thought. This effort to foster change, however, as Williams wisely demonstrates, neither disproves nor destroys redemptive suffering (e.g., surrogacy schemes) in that the sticking point is the perception of suffering when it is encountered. Put differently, one can hope to remove suffering but still understand the current condition

---

8. See Cone, *The Cross and the Lynching Tree*, 70, over against being a second-order enterprise as Gordon Kaufman suggests in *An Essay on Theological Method*, 3rd ed. (1975; Atlanta, GA: Scholars Press, 1995).

9. See Williams, *Sisters in the Wilderness: The Challenge of Womanist God-Talk* (Maryknoll, NY: Orbis Books, 1995).

10. Cone, *The Cross and the Lynching Tree*, 74, 148, and 151.

of suffering as having some benefit. And as Cone suggests, "black religion comes out of suffering."[11] Such a stance might simply involve critique of both injustice and the limits of religion to effect change. Nonetheless, Cone would rather understand this synergistic symbol of suffering as both the most profound challenge and the most compelling apology for a life-affirming (Christian) faith. That is to say, the lynching tree expresses the need for the gospel message as well as its true substance, and the cross points out the promise of liberation from the lynching tree.[12] They—the cross and the lynching tree—are not the same, but they are mutually dependent and linked. Without this synergy, Cone fears, nihilism and absurdity cloud the faith and suffocate all liberating activism.

Amplified by Cone's attention to the synergistic relationship between the cross and the lynching tree is more than a hint of redemptive suffering. He denies this numerous times in *The Cross and the Lynching Tree*, yet the denial has only rhetorical value in that his perception of the role of the lynching tree, as with the cross, involves a moment of meaning making with transformative effect. Cone writes, "Black Christians sang, 'Surely He Died on Calvary,' as if they were actually there. They felt something redemptive about Jesus' cross—transforming a cruel tree into a 'Wondrous Cross.' Blacks pleaded, 'Jesus Keep Me near the Cross,' because 'Calvary,' in a mysterious way they could not explain, was their redemption from the terror of the lynching tree."[13] Linking the lynching tree to the cross does not explain away human suffering but rather it highlights the Christian perception of suffering as a mechanism of change. The embodied and persistent nature of human suffering combined with a continuing sense of a God with a liberating agenda demands a compromise. God cannot be perceived as demonic, and the reality and nature of black suffering cannot be sidestepped or ignored. Hence, suffering must have some type of benefit. Williams and Jones recognize this dilemma and seek to provide an alternative by rethinking the nature of the Christ event—Williams as an ethical prompt and Jones as a nonconsequential superstition. Cone holds to a fuller story of Christ despite this unavoidable dilemma.

PAIN OR PAYMENT?

I end with an interesting observation: although the prosperity gospel message is disparaged as useless with respect to sociopolitical and economic injustice, it is one of the few approaches to the African American Christian faith that does not collapse

---

11. Ibid., 91–92 and 105. I have argued that embedded in this reasoning is an ethical dilemma, a posture toward the conditions of life that make sustained activity against moral evil difficult at best. See Pinn, *Why, Lord? Suffering and Evil in Black Theology* (New York, NY: Continuum, 1995).

12. Cone, *The Cross and the Lynching Tree*, 161.

13. Ibid., 73.

into redemptive suffering. This, to be sure, is not an apology for the prosperity gospel.[14] To the contrary, I would suggest that its more robust response to human suffering speaks to the tragic nature of the Christian faith and the fundamental flaw in the faith's ability to articulate an adequate response to human suffering vis-à-vis moral evil that does not collapse on itself. That is to say, prosperity serves as a modality of existence not gained through suffering but rather through the production of comfort and stability. Anything less than this situation of ease is considered nonbiblical and inconsistent with the deep meaning of the gospel message.

This is a different take—one deserving some scholarly attention—but no more beneficial. In either case, a compromise is reached. For the redemptive suffering proponent, embodied life is measured through pain that is experienced as a marker of righteous struggle, and for the prosperity gospel proponent, the fulfillment of human life lacks any real critique of the complex sources of oppression. Redemptive suffering theories by and large recognize the causes of oppression but respond in ways that measure life in terms of the feeling of this oppression, and the prosperity gospel seeks short-term resolutions that are consistent with the mechanics of life within the structures giving rise to oppression.

Both approaches raise a series of important questions: Has African American Christianity reached a point at which its inability to forge a liberated existence is undeniable? Is African American Christianity—conservative or liberal—merely a framework for survival within an absurd world, a venue for survival that requires believers to surrender their full humanity? Responses to moral evil as black suffering make these questions evident but provide little in the way of satisfying answers, that is, unless one finds glory in the embrace of suffering.

It is my position that a humanist, nontheistic response, one devoid of attention to transhistorical and supernatural claims and assumptions, is the best response to human suffering. I say this because it avoids the dilemma of redemptive suffering and maintains the centrality and integrity of embodied black bodies as the best measure of any theological response to misery. Furthermore, a humanist approach—even a humanist theology—maintains an awareness of the substance of suffering but in ways that also maintain the need for human accountability and responsibility.[15] In addition, this humanist take on moral evil assures measured realism with respect to the outcome of struggle against injustice. Rather than the rhetoric of liberation that

---

14. Interesting treatments related to this topic and connected issues include Milmon F. Harrison, *Righteous Riches: The Word of Faith Movement in Contemporary African American Religion* (New York, NY: Oxford University Press, 2005); Shayne Lee, *T. D. Jakes: America's New Preacher* (New York, NY: New York University Press, 2007); Stephanie Y. Mitchem, *Name It and Claim It? Prosperity Preaching in the Black Church* (Cleveland, OH: Pilgrim, 2007); and Jonathan L. Walton, *Watch This! The Ethics and Aesthetics of Black Televangelism* (New York, NY: New York University Press, 2009).

15. See Pinn, *The End of God-Talk: An African American Humanist Theology* (New York, NY: Oxford University Press, 2012).

is drawn from the cross, a nontheistic, humanist interpretation can recognize the importance of struggle but also the manner in which outcomes are not guaranteed. Instead, this approach suggests that the importance of our struggles to promote the integrity of life is found in the very struggles themselves. This theological approach to ethics recognizes the need to fight against injustice in light of the ever-present threat of failure. It avoids the hyperoptimism of the approach to moral evil available through black and womanist theologies, yet it also avoids the creation of a paradox in which the suffering generated by moral evil is both a problem to be fought and a necessity to be embraced. This humanist take on moral evil offers an opportunity to recognize the complex nature of human interactions without collapsing into cosmic justifications and explanations. And while some skeptics might suggest that this promotes nihilism and a defeatist attitude, I disagree. I am ever mindful of the words Lorraine Hansberry uses in *A Raisin in the Sun* when Beneatha is speaking with her mother: "Mama, you don't understand. It's all a matter of ideas, and God is just one idea I don't accept. It's not important. I am not going out and be immoral or commit crimes because I don't believe in God. I don't even think about it. It's just that I get tired of Him getting credit for all the things the human race achieves through its own stubborn effort. There simply is no blasted God—there is only man and it is he who makes miracles!"[16]

---

16. Hansberry, *A Raisin in the Sun: A Drama in Three Acts* (New York, NY: Random House, 1959), 36.

14 Evil, the New Atheism, and the God of the Trinity

by JACOB H. FRIESENHAHN

Recently, the so-called Four Horsemen of the New Atheism lost one of their members, as Christopher Hitchens succumbed to esophageal cancer in December of 2011. Although the remaining horsemen—Richard Dawkins, Daniel Dennett, and Sam Harris—often irritate more than intrigue, with their crass materialism and strident rejection of all things religious, I always found Hitchens too fascinating to ignore. His spirited challenges to Christian theism, both in his book *god is Not Great*[1] and in his numerous public lectures and debates, continue to shape my theological reflections. While perhaps no less a materialist and certainly no less a critic of religion than the other popular New Atheists, Hitchens was clearly a man of letters, a gifted writer, a formidable debater, and a public intellectual with an impressively quick wit. What I admired most about Hitchens was his consuming sense of justice and his sense of moral outrage. As a polemicist and controversialist par excellence, Hitchens tirelessly sought to demand justice whenever and wherever he found it wanting.

Some theists, especially those of a more academic stripe, scoff at the fad of New Atheism. They speak of its intellectual inferiority and draw unflattering comparisons between today's atheist celebrities and past philosophical giants of atheism, such as Arthur Schopenhauer, Ludwig Feuerbach, Friedrich Nietzsche, Karl Marx, and Sigmund Freud. Nonetheless, I suspect that what many theists, including many Christians, find troubling about the New Atheism are not the questions that can too easily be answered but those questions that, if we are honest, we struggle to answer or simply cannot answer. In this regard, I find several of Hitchens's favorite attacks on

---

1. Hitchens, *god is Not Great: How Religion Poisons Everything* (New York, NY: Twelve, 2009).

Christian theism to be noteworthy and, as I will highlight, many of his best polemics against religion return in various ways to one core issue: the problem of evil.

During a debate held at the March 2009 Christian Book Expo in Dallas, Texas, Hitchens sat on a panel with four Christian apologists: William Lane Craig, Douglas Wilson, Lee Strobel, and Jim Denison. The moderator of the debate, himself also a Christian, spoke of his struggles with cerebral palsy and suggested that Christianity offers great consolation to those who suffer. He then wondered what the highbrow, intellectual atheism of Hitchens could offer to the suffering. Hitchens responded by telling the story of an Austrian woman who was abused by her father over the course of twenty-four years and posed a series of questions to his Christian interlocutors. How can the Christian justify such terror as part of God's plan? How can the Christian justify heaven's indifference to such suffering? Is the Christian answer merely a glib supposition that this woman will have, in Hitchens's words, "a better time next time," as heaven somehow makes good all the horrors that happen here below, such that the divine permission thereof is morally sound after all?

Of Hitchens's Christian interlocutors, I found Wilson's response most valuable. Wilson spoke of hope in the face of evil and of the ultimate victory of justice. Far from justifying the violence performed against the woman in question, he explained, the Christian regards such abuse as evil and sinful (categories that may or may not be available to the atheist). Further, and more importantly, the Christian does not seek to *justify* the evil under discussion but rather trusts in God's power to overcome and annihilate it. The Christian response to the problem of evil, which is often called a "defense" or a "theodicy" depending upon its logical framework and structure, should never be a matter of defending evil. The Christian response to evil must instead entail a theology and praxis of hope in which all evil is condemned as such and the divine promise to abolish evil and establish justice is proclaimed.

But what is the properly theological foundation for such a response, a response that seeks not to justify evil in light of a divine plan but seeks to resist and overcome evil in light of divine justice? My contention is that the doctrine of the Trinity provides the most fruitful foundation from which to defend the justice of God in the face of evil and to announce hope to suffering humanity. In developing this argument I will draw deeply on the insights of the great twentieth-century Swiss theologian Hans Urs von Balthasar, particularly from those texts in which the connections between Trinity and theodicy are most explicitly considered, *Mysterium Paschale* and the final two volumes of von Balthasar's masterful Theo-Drama series.[2]

Von Balthasar's theology of the Trinity relies heavily on the concept of kenotic or self-giving love. The Greek word *kenosis* indicates an "emptying" or "pouring out."

2. Von Balthasar, *Mysterium Paschale: The Mystery of Easter*, trans. Aidan Nichols (Edinburgh, UK: Clark, 1990); *The Action*, Theo-Drama 4, trans. Graham Harrison (San Francisco, CA: Ignatius, 1994); and *The Last Act*, Theo-Drama 5, trans. Graham Harrison (San Francisco, CA: Ignatius, 1998).

The most significant single biblical referent for the Christian concept of kenosis is Philippians 2:5–7, which uses the verb form of the term: "Let the same mind be in you that was in Christ Jesus, who, though he was in the form of God, did not regard equality with God as something to be exploited, but *emptied* himself, taking the form of a slave, being born in human likeness" (NRSV, emphasis added). Von Balthasar speaks of Christ's kenosis as the Eternal Son's emptying of himself to become incarnate or human, even to the limit of accepting death on the cross and descending into hell. What is striking about the theology of von Balthasar is that he uses this idea of kenosis as the hermeneutical or interpretive key for understanding not only Christ, the Incarnate Son, but the very inner nature or life of God.

In von Balthasar's theology, the doctrine of the Trinity most fundamentally means that God's essence is an eternal interplay of kenotic love. The dynamic love at the heart of God is the sort of love by which lovers give themselves away for the sake of the beloved. This central idea of self-donation is more than an abstract concept; it is a term brimming with existential content. The experience of authentic love, the feeling of pouring oneself out for the sake of another, cuts to the heart of human existence. This lived experience of self-sacrificial love can provide a means for our deeper understanding of the Trinity. In the context of classical theism, the guiding analogy for approaching the Trinity may have been the threefold nature of the soul, that is, the soul itself, the soul's self-knowledge, and the soul's self-love. This rather closed-in *intra*personal model is perhaps best replaced by a more *inter*personal approach, in which we conceive of the triune life of God less in terms of the essential operations within an individual soul and more in terms of reciprocal loving relations and communion among distinct persons. Our guiding analogies for understanding the God of the Trinity can become the human family or community—human relations of love and reciprocity—not merely the interior life of the soul, which is often conceived along Platonic or Neoplatonic lines.

For von Balthasar, the content of the doctrine of the Trinity is essentially nothing other than "God is love" (see 1 John 4:8 and 4:16). At its root, the doctrine of the Trinity means that interpersonal love—love selflessly shared among distinct persons—is the very nature of God. In von Balthasar's theology of the Trinity, the Father begets or generates the Son in an act of self-emptying love. This outpouring of love is so primordial and constitutive both of God's essence and of God's relation to the world that von Balthasar speaks of the Father's begetting of the Son as the act of *supra-kenosis* or *Ur-kenosis* which undergirds all other acts of love, both divine and human: the Father utterly pours himself out, entrusting his very being and divine essence to the Son, letting go not only of all that he *has* but also of all that he *is* in his generation of the Son. The Son, in an act of total, reciprocal self-giving love, returns himself fully to the Father. The Father's perfect gift of love and total gift of himself to the Son elicits or engenders the fully matching or mirroring kenotic love of the Son. All that the Son has and is he receives only from the Father, and the Son returns himself without remainder to the Father in a perpetual act of filial love and trust. The Holy Spirit is the personal expression, the We, of this personal, primordial exchange of pure love, such that the Father and Son stand in an I-Thou relation to one another, while the Holy Spirit is the We, or the Spirit of communal love shared between the I-Thou of Father-Son.

In a world of individualism, the doctrine of the Trinity confronts us with a God whose nature is social and communal. In a world of consumerism, consumption, and the grasping of the ego, the properly Christian view of God as triune envisions the divine essence as a life of love in service only of the Other, a life in which every I prefers the welfare of the Thou over and above all self-interest. The consuming individual ego, so much taken for granted in the modern West, is the very opposite of God's nature as revealed to us by the doctrine of the Trinity. While sinful humankind seeks modes of domination—the assertion of one's will-to-power over against any competing factors—the truth of the Trinity shows us another way. In the life of God, the life of the Trinity, into which we are all called as our final destiny and beatitude, we discover love that lets go, forgoes power, and puts oneself at the disposal of the Other.

The *immanent* Trinity, God's own eternal inner nature considered in and of itself, is expressed historically in the *economic* Trinity, which is the self-revelation of God as manifested in salvation history. I have primarily discussed the inner life of God, but Christians believe that God's nature is expressed or revealed historically, through salvation history and what is often called the economy of salvation. Indeed, the entire life, death, and resurrection of Jesus Christ, the Incarnate Son, reveals the inner nature of the Triune God.

At the base of the Mount of Olives at a place called Gethsemane, Christ throws himself on the ground and prays, "My Father, if it is possible, let this cup pass from me; yet not what I want but what you want" (Matt. 26:39) and shortly after, "My Father, if this cannot pass unless I drink it, your will be done" (Matt. 26:42). These prayers from Son to Father reveal not merely the man Jesus beseeching God but rather the Incarnate Son in relation to his Father. The deepest context of the prayers of Christ at Gethsemane is the Trinity. The Incarnate Son, in the face of great suffering, indeed in the face of accepting all evil onto or into himself, prostrates himself before his Father and prays "your will be done." Christ entrusts or gives himself to the will of God the Father, both within salvation history and eternally in the life or dynamism of the immanent Trinity.

In the Gospels of Matthew and Mark, Jesus's sole words from the cross are "My God, my God, why have you forsaken me?" (Matt. 27:46; cf. Mark 15:34). This cry of abandonment comes from the opening line of Psalm 22, and thus Jesus's prayer must be interpreted in the tradition of the faith of Israel. Once more, we do not merely behold the man Jesus crying out in anguish to God. Instead, in the context of the Trinity, what we discover is no less than the paradox of God Incarnate confessing his Godforsakenness. If Christ is not merely human but also divine, how then can God experience abandonment by God? The answer lies only in the mystery of the Trinity. God the Son through his full solidarity with sinful humanity has entered into the deepest reality of sin—alienation from God—such that the Son experiences separation from the Father. For von Balthasar, such *economic* separation, that is, separation of Father and Son within salvation history in the event of the cross, is possible only as grounded in the *immanent* Trinity, that is, in the infinite distance among the divine persons eternally present within God's inner nature.

The grounding of Gethsemane and the cross in the Trinity and the implications of these events for our salvation are made more clear through the sacraments of the church and in the Eucharist above all others. Christ gives himself completely to us, humbles himself so as to be present under the forms of bread and wine, and entrusts himself fully in his body, blood, soul, and divinity to humanity for the sake of our salvation. Christ's gift of self upon the cross, the sacrifice of his body, and the shedding of his blood make possible the breaking of the bread and the sharing of the cup, which become sacramentally nothing less than the gift of the body and blood of Christ. This sacrament of Holy Communion draws us through the self-sacrifice of Christ into the *communio* of the inner life of God, the communio of the Holy Trinity. The sacramental reality of the church as a whole, the mystical body of Christ, subsists within the triune nature of God. The many members of the church can dwell together as one body only within the context of participation in God's trinitarian being, in which the three divine persons dwell together in the one divine essence. The communal reality of God's own nature is the foundation for the life of the church.

At this point, we can begin to perceive the contours of the Christian and trinitarian answer that I would like to propose in response to the problem of evil. Rather than relying on the largely pat answers of the free-will defense (the argument that God must permit evil so as to leave intact human moral freedom), the notion of some necessary balance between good and evil, or the claim that all suffering is a test didactically provided by God, the theodicy of the Trinity reveals that human suffering, united to the cross and to the descent of Christ into hell, becomes a gateway into the life of the Triune God and a gateway through which evil is annihilated and suffering and death are transformed. The broken relationship between humanity and God (due to sin) is undone in the spiritual space of the perfect relationship of love between Father and Son; it is undone by the power of the Holy Spirit. Human suffering and death, when united by divine grace to the suffering and death of Jesus Christ, become not only conformed to Christ but also thereby brought up into the transforming life of the Trinity. Sin-conditioned suffering and death become converted—through the incarnation and the paschal mystery—into the kenotic love and life of self-abandonment that is the Trinity.

I must clarify what I am proposing by delineating what I am not proposing. I am not justifying the maltreatment of human persons as a strange way of rendering said persons closer to God. I am not giving any spiritual or religious excuse for cruelty toward human persons, or toward any sentient life for that matter. Nor am I providing theological warrant for neglect or indifference toward those who are undergoing great anguish. I am not suggesting that a person caught in a situation of abuse ought to accept his or her abuse as the will of God and thus as a situation not to be fought or escaped. I do not assume that a victim of horrendous evil, one who has been broken down or disintegrated physically or psychologically, will be able to or called upon by God to make an active or self-conscious use of his or her suffering for spiritual advancement. Rather, my point, which includes an eschatological dimension, is that God himself redeems, in Christ by the cross and within the life of the Trinity, all forms of human suffering. It must be said, especially today when the entire enterprise of theodicy often comes under great suspicion—and not without reason—that the goal of a properly Christian theodicy is to proclaim hope to all who are suffering and to proclaim a hope that is clearly grounded in the mystery of the God of Jesus Christ. Far from endorsing abuse or neglect, the theodicy suggested by the von Balthasar's theology of the Trinity ought to inspire us to bring God's transforming grace into every evil so that the world may be restored through Christ in the embrace of the Triune God.

But let us return to Christopher Hitchens. Have I really answered his challenge? Hitchens, of course, was aware that the traditional Christian answer to the problem of evil points toward the figure of Jesus Christ on the cross; however, he regarded the very notion of vicarious atonement as itself immoral. Hitchens liked to say that one person can pay another's debt or serve another's jail term but for one person to take away the personal moral responsibility of another is an impossibility or, in any case, an immoral proposition.

That the one who offers to remove sin and guilt from our lives is not merely human but God Incarnate must be part of the Christian's reply to this objection, but perhaps an even better reply would be to note the profoundly *participatory* character of Christian redemption in the paschal event. The cross does not simply remove evil from the world in any superficial or unilateral sense. Indeed, human beings sin no less today than they did prior to the time of Christ. Suffering is just as omnipresent, death just as inevitable, and the all-too-human problems of guilt and anxiety remain with us as much now as ever. What then has the cross accomplished? As a past event, whereby salvation is merely accomplished on our behalf by someone else, perhaps the cross accomplished nothing—not to overstate the point. The true meaning of the cross draws us into the suffering, death, and the resurrection of Christ. It is not that we do not suffer; it is that we suffer with Christ or in Christ. Death still stands as (seemingly) the ultimate terror, but those who die in Christ also rise in Christ. In short, the nature of Christian salvation is as participatory as it is vicarious. Sin is abolished by the cross, and sin-conditioned suffering and death are transformed, but only by our active and participatory inclusion into the body of Christ and through Christ into the life of the Trinity.

Finally, I want to highlight perhaps the best of all of Hitchens's attacks upon the credibility of Christianity. Hitchens employed this argument more in his frequent live debates with Christian apologists than in the text of his *god is Not Great*; thus, in the summary just below, I paraphrase his case as best I can. Hitchens would set up this argument by first noting that human beings have apparently existed for roughly one hundred thousand years, though estimates of the exact time span vary. Given this vast time frame of human existence, to be a Christian means having to believe a most incredible story, namely that God simply watched humanity living in great misery—constantly at war, enduring a pitifully low average life expectancy, subject to famine and plague, ignorant of the workings of the surrounding world, forced to live in constant fear—for some ninety-eight thousand years. Then, after watching "with folded arms" for all that time, God finally decides, a mere two thousand years ago, that enough is enough. It is at last time to intervene. But how? By staging a "gruesome human sacrifice" in the "unlettered desert" of the Middle East. An innocent man is to be tortured to death, and *that* shall be the long overdue salvation of miserable humankind.

Even more than the notion of God watching indifferently or sadistically the travail of the world below, Hitchens often criticized the concept of God as "celestial dictator." God appears as the eternal supervising authority, the ultimate totalitarian ruler, always standing ready to convict us even of thought crimes. To paraphrase Hitchens's quip, God is a sort of heavenly and eternal Kim Jong Il. Furthermore, God cruelly creates humans as innately sick and then orders us under the pain of ultimate judgment and condemnation to be well.

Despite the frequency with which Hitchens seemed to repeat this polemic against God as dictator, I always found this particular aspect of his argument against Christian theism markedly weak. It is almost as if the Christian doctrine of God were formulated for the precise purpose of refuting this false concept of God, in relation to which we all ought to be atheists. The God of the Trinity, the God of interpersonal love, the God whose very essence is love selflessly shared among distinct persons, is the utter opposite of the image of God attacked by Hitchens, just as the God of the cross is the exact inverse of Hitchens's God who stands by with folded arms as we suffer. The Triune God does not create us as sick with the disease of sin; sin is instead the freely chosen condition into which we fall by pride, as famously dramatized in Genesis 3. Nor does God simply order us to make ourselves well, but in an act of ultimate *solidarity*—a key concept for Hitchens himself—the God of the Trinity enacts our redemption in the theo-drama of the cross.

Nonetheless, Hitchens's delightfully barbed parody or satire of the Christian story, I believe, constitutes a serious challenge to Christian faith in the face of evil. I maintain that the ninety-eight-thousand-years challenge can only be partially answered in terms of Christian theological reflection as it has been developed thus far. Thus, I want to conclude this short article with an open challenge. How do we account not only for the tens of thousands of years of human history prior to Christ, and indeed, prior to Abraham, but also for the millions of years of sentient life on this planet, life that has seemingly from the start been subject to pain, suffering, death, decay, predation, and parasitism? I am here invoking both the prehistory of humanity and the crucial question of natural evil. Christian theology, undertaken at the foot of the cross and within the framework of the Trinity, must address this daunting problem and must do so in terms that are coherent and cogent for theology in a post-Darwinian context.

15 Race, Criminality, and the Divine Occupation: An Interview with J. Kameron Carter

by DAVID KLINE

IN THIS INTERVIEW, THE theologian J. Kameron Carter discusses his current work regarding political theology and the construction of the modern racialized world. Carter speaks about the Obama presidency and the so-called post-racial moment, the recent Occupy movement, and the shooting of Trayvon Martin. He then reflects on theology's ongoing work in the wake of colonialism, framing theological education as a "criminal act."

The Other Journal (*TOJ*): As a presidential candidate and a president, Barack Obama has faced numerous accusations concerning his identity that throw his status as an "authentic" American into question. How might this shed light on the matter of race and identity in America?

J. Kameron Carter (JKC): Many of the things that Obama has been continually accused of in his presidency already announced themselves in the 2008 campaign. The question of his race and religiosity was put front and center in the Jeremiah Wright controversy, particularly because Wright was taken as a kind of synecdoche and symbol for black Christian theology, which, in the way it was talked about in the press, was deemed an abhorrent form of Christianity, precisely because of its radicalism. In that context, Obama had to put some distance between himself and Wright, and in response, he gave one of his most important speeches. It's packed full of interesting, illuminating, problematic things that are worth a great deal of reflection.

Then, in the midst of that debate, there is the rise of Sarah Palin. God forbid if I stay too long on Palin, but one way to understand her is as a kind of response to everything that Obama was being accused of lacking. If Obama was suspect as to his birth, she was not. If Obama was suspect as to his Christianity, she was the kind of quintessential representation of the evangelical Christian, and so on and so forth. I think that one of the reasons that John McCain was pressed to bring Palin onto the ticket as his vice-presidential candidate was because she was the symbolic response to Obama.

What you have here is a contest of Christianities. The presidency itself became a staging ground: the campaign for the presidency, for the political space of the presidency and what the president symbolically represents for the nation, became a "sight," as in a way to see, and a "site," as in a way to locate our great anxiety over the meaning of Christianity in the present conjuncture. Simply because Obama was elected doesn't mean these issues have been put to rest. The proof is the Tea Party movement, which is a kind of refraction of what Palin represents. And so, ever since Obama has been in the presidency, he and his presidency have continually been on trial.

Here I can't help but reference the killing of seventeen-year-old Trayvon Martin of Sanford, Florida. There have been national protests and a great deal of international attention on this incident, with cries minimally for George Zimmerman's arrest as a start toward justice for Martin and social justice in the land.[1] But beyond this there are deeper, extralegal factors because much of modern law presupposes them. To explain what I mean, consider President Obama's one guarded comment in response to the killing. Obama was guarded in his response for at least two reasons. One, race has been a spectral presence in his presidency, and every time that specter has made an appearance, there's been trouble. There was the Wright incident in the campaign, the Shirley Sherrod incident, and the famous "beer summit" in the wake of Harvard professor Henry Louis Gates Jr.'s unwarranted arrest in his Boston home. Each of these incidents spelled trouble for the Obama presidency. He was damned if he dealt with them and damned if he didn't. The second reason he was guarded was that it was still an open case and there was still an ongoing investigation.

At a press conference shortly after the issue went national, Obama said that his heart went out to the parents of Martin over what had happened to their son, and then he said something most telling. He said that if he had had a son, his son would look like Trayvon Martin. This is a powerful statement. While calling for the law to work with deliberate speed, he shifted from the register of law to the register of representation; his comment suggested that this incident is a moment within a wider event and crisis.

I call it the crisis of the gaze or what one scholar has called a problem of "the right to look." That is, in our society, who has the right to look and at what and

---

1. Zimmerman was arrested and charged with second-degree murder on April 11, 2012.

whom?[2] Furthermore, that gaze is one of violence. This gaze, which I call *iconicity*, visualizes some people as the normal, as the proper citizen, and others as improper citizens (at best) or noncitizens or criminal (at worst). Martin was caught within this icon-onomy—and the law itself participates in this icon-onomy; the law is not anterior or posterior to the icon-onomy or the logic of looking. The hoodie, as an item of clothing, was the flashpoint. The hoodie communicated to the one with the right to look (and thus the supposed right to judge) that what was being looked at was a criminal, not just in his activity but in his being (his very existence was criminal). But why just a hoodie? There are many folks who wear hoodies, including white folks. I suggest that the hoodie was a kind of prosthetic, an extension of Martin's blackness. That is to say, it's the equation *hoodie + blackness = criminal being* that we saw enacted in the Trayvon Martin incident. And thus, the hoodie became on Martin's body a signifier of blackness and thus of criminal being. When Obama said that if he had a son that son would look like Martin, I believe it is this problem he was gesturing toward. And so, among the many kinds of problems that are associated with this killing, legal among them, it's also a problem of the icon and the gaze.

Patristic thinkers like John of Damascus, Theodore the Studite, and Patriarch Nicephorus of Constantinople taught that icons train us how to see, how to look at the world. My claim is that blackness in modernity functions as an icon. It has been mobilized to train us—to train the Zimmermans of the world, indeed, all of us—how to *look* at the world. I suggest that that look is both *in* and already *inside of* an economy of social violence, which authorizes itself with the force of something like divine authority. In the modern situation, the situation that we are all trapped inside of, race—blackness—will find you if you're black, just like it found Martin. That's the point. Obama knows that. If Obama didn't know it when he got into the presidency, he surely knows it now. My work has been to reckon with the fact that this problem I've been describing has been mediated by a certain vision of Christian faith, a vision of faith that I take to be a profound distortion of Christianity. Therefore, a big part of my work is to analyze this problem and, by working through it, to imagine what it would look like to think of Christianity beyond itself, to think of Christianity after Christianity.

TOJ: And I assume that to think beyond or after Christianity does not mean to think post-racially?

JKC: It doesn't mean thinking post-racially because that implies we are beyond race. In the 1960s and 1970s, the work of Martin Luther King Jr., Malcolm X, Angela Davis,

---

2. See Nicholas Mirzoeff, *The Right to Look: A Counterhistory of Visuality* (Durham, NC: Duke University Press, 2011).

and many others included a sense that maybe we could realize some of the great goals and ambitions that were put on the cultural, national, and even international table around race matters. But in the 1980s those gestures were commandeered and taken over by the political and cultural right such that hard-core conservatives now make the case that staying true to capitalist sensibilities will help us realize universality in equality and freedom. In many ways we could say that when Obama showed up on the presidential scene, he became a kind of cipher through which people could project the kind of completion and culmination of that earlier cultural wish to be beyond race. But what does it mean to be beyond race, and what does the wish to be beyond it signify? In my work, I attempt to show that this means, in some sense, the completion and fulfillment of a Kantian project: universality.

The discourse of the universal is a very particularist discourse. It is the discourse in which whiteness completes itself and, therefore, no longer needs to refer to itself as white. As I said, Immanuel Kant already theorized the so-called post-racial as the completion of whiteness into true universality or globality.[3] Thus, what blacks (or Latinos and Latinas or Asians, etc.) must do is translate into and accommodate their wishes—their grievances—to the logic of the universal and jettison all this talk about blackness. If that happens, it will be the completion of the universal, the moment of the post-racial, and yet the post-racial, as a racial fantasy of the universal, is in fact the highest inflection of the racial.

TOJ: In an editorial published in the *Nation* back in March 2011, Melissa Harris-Perry wrote that "More and more Americans are learning what it feels like to be unsafe and unprotected. In other words they're learning what it's like to be black." Since then, we have seen the Occupy Wall Street movement and its various forms across the country organize against the prevailing forces of the Washington–Wall Street financial complex. Although the movement certainly includes people of color, it has been projected largely as a contingent of young white people. How do you see the Occupy movement as it relates to the history of race in this country? How do you interpret it in the wake of the 2008 campaign and the Obama presidency? How might we interpret the movement theologically?

JKC: These are all vital questions, and I've been thinking a lot about the Occupy movement. Last December I was given the opportunity to preach on Christmas Day, and the Gospel lectionary passage was from Luke chapter 2, the birth of Christ. I titled the sermon "Christmas: God's Occupy Movement." What I tried to do was

---

3. I'm hard at work on a book, *The Secular Jesus: Political Theology from Columbus to the Age of Obama* (Yale University Press), that shows how a similar logic informs the founding statements of the United States. The figure I'm currently taking up in this regard is Thomas Jefferson, the third president of the United States.

use the Christmas moment to frame the Occupy movement in theological terms, to frame it in terms of the work of Christ, the person of Christ, the identity of Jesus. One of the things that I meditated on was the first thing the angels tell the shepherds in the story: that this baby shall be called "the Savior, Christ the Lord." The angel says to the shepherds that the sign, the proof shall we say, that you have found the one I'm talking about is that you will find him in an animal trough, in a manger. This is the one who is going to be "God with us," who is going to be the Savior, Christ the Lord. What I was trying to do in the sermon was to talk about what it means for God to become a creature in our condition, to come among us in a particular position—the position of the slave. He enters into slaveism, enters into the condition of a slaveocricy, and in that condition meets us as the one who will save, the one who will bring healing, the one who will restore us from our brokenness; he will be Christ. To say he will be the Christ under the conditions of Roman imperial rule is to say that he will enter into the problematic of empire, the problematic of imperialism, and politically disrupt it. That this one will be the Lord also means that he will be a new articulation of what lordship is about, a new articulation of what mastery is about. He will explode the ideas of mastery and the logics of lordship in relationship to the projects of bondage. This is who Jesus is. Now, where will you find this one? Do not go to the halls of power to find this one. To find this one, you must go to where the animals drink their water. This is where the beginning of God's occupation occurs.

Now when we think about that in relationship to the Occupy movement of today, we must remember that the movement leaps off not from those so-called Christian zones but from the zones of Arab life: Egypt, Tunisia, Syria. The events in these places are what ignited what we now call the global Occupy movement. How do we think about this? What does this signify? I think Professor Harris-Perry is right on point when she says that the Occupy movement is a kind of window into how close, shall we say, the 99 percent are to the conditions of abjection, to the conditions of the black. The truth of the matter is that most people are not far from that. But she's also right—and this may be quite difficult to think through—that it's not quite the condition of being black.

Interestingly, the Occupy movement might be thought of as in some ways analogous to the Tea Party movement—not at the level of their political and cultural demands, of course, but the two movements are analogous inasmuch as they both rise from a subject position within a particular political space, especially as the Occupy movement, which began as the Arab Spring, translates itself into the West. If we make a distinction between the Arab Spring and the Occupy movement in America, then this translation becomes a transition into, as you say, a space where disaffected young white folks make their political demands known. It is in this regard that the Occupy movement and the Tea Party movement are very much the same. Both emerge from a particular subject position in which there is a citizen who can air grievances and make political and cultural demands to political constituencies that are pressed to respond. As far as that's the case, and if we stick with Professor Harris-Perry, in many ways that's a reality that is distinctly white.

TOJ: This presses into what the film theorist Frank B. Wilderson calls the "nonontology" of slave being.[4] Slaveness is both a historical category and an indicator of being in which certain bodies are always already outside of the social and cultural privileges of citizen subjectivity. And so we might say that the Occupy movement in America has not grappled with the deepest ontological realities of slaveness and blackness.

JKC: Rather than grappling with the problematics of being—the problem of subject positions in which being is constituted as nonbeing—the Occupy movement has not questioned the ontological frame that always already determines black being as nonbeing. That's what I think Professor Harris-Perry is gesturing toward. We cannot collapse the Occupy movement into the grievances that the slave calls for. We cannot collapse the cries of the Occupy movement into the cries of dereliction. Those are two different cries. The Occupy movement says, "I want what is my due, given the way that I am positioned within the ontological frame," whereas the slave cry, the cry of dereliction, says that there is no space in the ontological frame whatsoever for me.

One theorist who I've been reading a lot of lately is Denise Ferreira da Silva who wrote a very important book called *Toward a Global Idea of Race*.[5] She gives a profound analysis of modernity as a horizon of death where she thinks from the vantage of the death-bound subject within the ontological frame. Within this frame—the space of the plantation system—there are no grievances that the slave can place before the master. What would it mean for a slave to come up to the master and say, "I want my due, and until I get my due, I'm going to occupy this plantation"? And so the slave exists under a commuted death sentence. Slave being is death deferred, and that deferment can be revoked at any moment. I think the Occupy movement has given us a lot of very serious issues to deal with, but this is a level of analysis into which it isn't prepared to descend.

TOJ: What do you have to say about the work of theology in all of this, specifically in terms of Christian formation? Is it even possible for theology to offer a way forward given its own implication in the construction of the ontological space of the plantation system?

4. Wilderson, *Red, White, and Black: Cinema and the Structure of US Antagonisms* (Durham, NC: Duke University Press, 2010), 5.

5. Ferreira da Silva, *Toward a Global Idea of Race* (Minneapolis, MN: University of Minnesota Press, 2007).

JKC: That's a great question that gets to the heart of why I do what I do. I've been turning to two thinkers in modern theology who I think are vital here: Karl Barth and Dietrich Bonhoeffer. What both Barth and Bonhoeffer understood was that given Christian theology's implicatedness in the construction of the modern world, the work of theological education could not go on the way that it had. Moreover, they both understood that there was no template out there to tell us where to go from this place of implicatedness. We might look to various thinkers of the Christian tradition, but we can't simply repeat them. I think this is perhaps more clear in Bonhoeffer than in Barth—Barth had a longer trajectory of scholarly and intellectual output than did Bonhoeffer, and with the way in which Barth executed his task, it's easy to misinterpret his message as "Retrieve the tradition," in the same way that people misinterpret me as just trying to resuscitate orthodoxy. But I think both men understood that theological education had to rethink itself, and in realizing that, they found themselves bumping up against a particular mode of theological education that could not speak to the social realities unfolding around them.

Bonhoeffer in particular had come to understand that theological education and Christian formation, that is, discipleship, had been so tethered to reinforcing the order of things that the only persons theological education could produce were pastors and leaders who raised their hands and saluted with the "Heil Hitler." He thus tried an experiment: the seminary at Finkenwalde, which was a vision of theological education as a kind of eschatological act, an act done in light of a future yet to come.[6] Theological education, he believed, was a participation in the work of Jesus Christ, a work that always exceeds us and is more than us, a work that always happens within—if I may use an awkward phrase—"a receiving future," a future that must be received, a future that is always interrogating us and that is therefore always calling us to the prayerful posture of repentance. This horizon of futurity, of receptivity, is routed through concrete, enfleshed persons in all of their particularities; the Christian is always receiving himself or herself in the very relationship with the Other.

The modern world that I've been narrating, which produces the analytics of raciality and the production of this particular thing called Man—split between *homo religiosis* and *homo dominatus*, between the proper Christian and the improper exterior savage—is the result of theological education. Now, if we ever got our heads around what that means—and pardon the language—that should scare the shit out of us! It should terrify us because it means that when we're sitting in a classroom learning the doctrine of the Trinity or reading our Thomas Aquinas or Augustine, we are inside a historical framework of domination. But what should we do? If we choose not to shut down the institution called the seminary, what else can we do?

---

6. See Bonhoeffer, *Life Together* (New York, NY: Harper and Row, 1954).

What worries me is that there are still too many theological thinkers who have not dealt with what this really means or how it should change how we do our work. And so the first thing I think we have to learn from people like Barth and Bonhoeffer is that we must come to terms with that reality—it must rock us to the core. Until that happens, the work of theology will always be suspect. Again, as I think about Bonhoeffer's itinerary, Finkenwalde is the crucial moment. At Finkenwalde Bonhoeffer is recasting theological education in terms of what I am calling Christian fugitivity. Remember, what Bonhoeffer is doing at Finkenwalde is a criminal act. The Hitler regime ordered that Finkenwalde be closed down, and so all the seminarians there were de facto criminals. This made theological education a matter of life and death; it pushed the one who dared pursue theological education in proximity to criminality—and this is well worth thinking about. In this way, criminality becomes the new modality of theological formation. What does it mean to form ministers who do not go with the order of things but who represent, because they follow Jesus, an interruption of the order of things? That's the question that Bonhoeffer performs out for us.

TOJ: We might say that the criminality you are identifying in Bonhoeffer has profound connections to the classic slave narratives in which resistance to the conditions of slave being happen by the slave essentially becoming a criminal or a fugitive. How might we connect what you've just described as "Christian fugitivity" with these narratives?

JKC: In speaking of Christian fugitivity, I'm talking about when Harriet Jacobs, in *Incidents in the Life of a Slave Girl*, goes up into the garret, into the rooftop attic, and has to hide there for seven years.[7] She frames her hiding as an entrance into the zone of Holy Saturday, into the entombment of Jesus Christ, where she escapes and becomes a fugitive. Jacobs is a runaway slave who is trying to escape from her master, Dr. Norcom, who wanted to rape her because she was a beautiful black woman, and like so many black women slaves, her body was gazed upon as available for all modalities of death, including social death by way of rape. So she runs away and hides in the garret of her grandmother's house for seven years to keep watch over her children until she can surreptitiously arrange for them to escape to the North. Inside the garret space of fugitivity—the space of slave being as criminal being—she's trying to work out what it means to be, in effect, a follower of Jesus and to stand up for what it means for her to be a creature of God.

In speaking of Christian fugitivity, I'm talking about when Henry Box Brown climbed inside a box with the help of a few black friends, who poked two holes in

---

7. See Henry Louis Gates Jr., ed., *The Classic Slave Narratives* (New York, NY: Signet Classics, 2002), 437–668.

the box so he could breathe, and he mailed himself to the city of Philadelphia. Brown became a fugitive; that box became the zone of imprisonment, the place of an impossible subjectivity. It became the zone in which he broke the rules of the order of things. And it was inside that zone of criminality in which something else was being worked out. That's the air pocket that I mentioned in my earlier interview with *The Other Journal*, signified by the resurrection of Jesus Christ.[8] And what Bonhoeffer's doing is something very similar. I want to read Bonhoeffer in relationship to this transatlantic new performance of black being. In light of this, theological education has a lot of work to do, and people like Barth and Bonhoeffer perhaps offer some resources for us to think about our contemporary moment. But even with Barth and Bonhoeffer, as well as other theological voices, we're going to have to upgrade and tweak them, because they don't say everything that needs to be said. I don't want to valorize their positions; they're simply conversation partners for this contemporary moment—I'm not trying to step back to their moment.

TOJ: Are you suggesting that the only way forward for the work of Christian theology in the wake of modernity is to learn to think theologically from the positions and perspectives of the slave, the illegal, the criminal, the immigrant, and the fugitive?

JKC: Right, but the point here is not a valorization, shall we say, of the position of the black as such. Why should we look to the position of the black, to the position of the slave? We should look to it because that's where God, in Jesus, has looked. It's a christological move, a christological zone, a christological space. Social space and the logics of space come to be reconfigured in the horizon of Jesus, and where that takes place is not in this kind of zone called universal man. Universal man is nothing but a discourse of the white subject. That's not where we live. We look, according to Philippians 2, to the impossible place of the slave, to the *doulos*, because that's where God looked and where God meets us and has met us. This God, Emmanuel, has met us in the impossible place, the place of nonbeing within the terms of the order of things. To be in this place of nonbeing is to be at the cross, but in Jesus, it is also to be in his resurrection.

---

8. See Brown, *Narrative of the Life of Henry Box Brown* (New York, NY: Oxford University Press, 2002); and David Kline, "Race, Theology, and the Politics of Abjection: An Interview with J. Kameron Carter, Part I," *The Other Journal* 20, http://theotherjournal.com/2012/03/26/race-theology-and-the-politics-of-abjection-an-interview-with-j-kameron-carter-part-i/.

16 Religious Activism, the Living Wage Movement, and Occupy Wall Street: An Interview with C. Melissa Snarr

by BRANDY DANIELS

When thinking about religious communities and progressive social justice work, many of us assume an oppositional relationship—perhaps we think of the church groups and activist organizations who protest gay pride parades or canvass neighborhoods to repeal Obamacare, or conversely, perhaps we think of activist organizations who blame Christianity for limitations on women's reproductive rights and who assume that Christianity is synonymous with conservatism. But today, organizations like Sojourners, Progressive Christians Uniting, and Muslims for Progressive Values are challenging these perceived dichotomies. In her book *All You That Labor*,[1] C. Melissa Snarr not only makes a case for the ways religious communities should have a voice in social justice work but also depicts how such communities are already making a difference, particularly in the living wage movement. In this interview, Snarr shares from these insights, draws connections between the living wage movement and Occupy Wall Street, and reflects theologically and ethically on the role of religious activism as a response to economic injustice.

The Other Journal (*TOJ*): I happened to read your book last fall, right as Occupy Wall Street was gaining momentum and media coverage. I was struck by the connections between Occupy Wall Street and the living wage movement—such as their discontent with increases in worker poverty and the declining purchasing power of minimum wage. In the final chapter of *All You That Labor*, you point to how the living wage

---

1. Snarr, *All You That Labor: Religion and Ethics in the Living Wage Movement* (New York, NY: New York University Press, 2011). Further references to this book will be in the form of parenthetical citations in the body of the interview.

movement is part of a larger struggle of a "participatory justice" that seeks to "build the moral agency of low-wage workers and their allies in order to alter the landscape of the political economy" (16). How might your reflections on the role of religious activism in the living wage movement speak to Occupy Wall Street?

C. Melissa Snarr (CMS): One of the things that is fascinating about Occupy Wall Street is that it is not perceived as a religious movement. Yes, there have certainly been religious actors involved—Serene Jones's November 16, 2011, *Huffington Post* piece on the around-the-clock chaplaincy that Union Theological Seminary is trying to do, for instance—but, from a media perspective, one does not typically connect Occupy Wall Street with religious activism. Interestingly, the same thing is true with the living wage movement. Part of why I was interested in writing *All You That Labor* is that the living wage movement is one of the few successful progressive movements in the last fifteen years, and although there is a lot of writing on it, hardly anything has been written about the religious actors who helped lead this movement. But if you look deeply at the story, the religious actors have a major presence. Thus, I think there are some interesting parallels to think about in terms of how religious activists are hidden in the world of economic activism.

Your question also gets at how the living wage movement is not just about the loss of economic agency. Yes, it's about the disparity of wealth, but the movement also argues that disparity of wealth and income is built on the erosion of *political* agency. And that's why we have this growing gap between the wealthy and the poor. I'm reminded of a December 16, 2011, *New York Times* article by Charles Blow that shows how it is actually harder in the United States to move from the lower quintiles to the upper quintiles than it is in Europe. The weakening of labor unions and the erosion of working-class power are factors of this lack of economic mobility in the United States. With Occupy Wall Street and the labor battles in Wisconsin, we're now beginning to see this intersection of economic and political agency more clearly. There are a lot of folks realizing: "Oh, all this is tied to campaign finance reform!" For example, Newt Gingrich's campaign was given a five million dollar contribution from a casino owner through a super PAC, something that wouldn't have been possible five years ago.[2] The intersection between things like campaign-finance reform and labor laws demonstrates to me that we cannot divorce the erosion of economic agency and mobility from political agency in the United States. That is where I think the living wage movement overlaps very strongly with Occupy Wall Street. Where are the voices of

---

2. Nicholas Confessore, "'Super PAC' for Gingrich to Get $5 Million Infusion," *New York Times*, January 23, 2012, http://www.nytimes.com/2012/01/24/us/politics/super-pac-for-gingrich-to-get-5-million-infusion.html. Since this interview, the billionaire Sheldon Adelson has given more "substantial" donations to Gingrich's super PAC, and later, to Mitt Romney's super PAC.

lower-income people in politics? There's really no need for them now because politics is controlled by a different set of economic interests and political actors.

TOJ: How do you see religious communities promoting and acknowledging this political agency? In your book, you note that one of the contributions of religious communities to these conversations is in "bridging social capital" (78). Given that this issue is on evil and late modernity, I'm curious about how religion can play a role in this particular political, economic, historical context. Is this one of the ways that religious communities can resist the neoliberal tactic of autonomy?

CMS: There are so many ways to get at that question. Although it has been more clear or more easily assumed in times past, recent research suggests that religious institutions are still a site for building civic and political skills and analyses of the material world.[3] This is especially true for folks who aren't necessarily getting these resources through pathways of higher education or the pathways of social capital that one would get from a professional field or something of that sort. Instead, the role that labor unions used to play (and still play in many other countries) for the working and lower classes, and for folks who are moving constantly in and out of poverty, is being played by religious institutions in the United States. In many struggling neighborhoods, religious institutions are not only one of the last sites of social capital but they also function as a place where leadership skills are developed. This latter point is enormously important, and it translates to political settings. A housekeeper at Vanderbilt might be leading his or her church council in North Nashville, which provides leadership opportunity and also cultivates an array of skills that can translate into political activism. There is also an irony here. The homogeneity of so many religious institutions—the fact that Sunday morning worship or Friday Shabbat service are some of the most racially and socioeconomically segregated spaces—while problematic, also enables leadership capacity and development in those settings for people who would normally not be cast for leadership in other (workplace) contexts.

On a different note, religious communities are valuable in fostering political agency because they provide another set of moral languages, analytical tools, imaginative options, and discourses. I don't mean that the church has its own discourse—I think that, for example, when we kneel in prayer, that it is also a political act that recalls bowing to a ruler, and there are many political hangovers in "Christian" practices. And I do not mean that church discourse achieves a purity that is lacking elsewhere. But there is enough space between the multiple discourses found in religious communities that those gaps can be played against each other; those gaps and those

---

3. See Robert D. Putnam and David E. Campbell, *American Grace: How Religion Divides and Unites Us* (New York, NY: Simon & Schuster, 2010).

leverage points are the places where we can have enough space to ask questions. For example, is this really the only way to picture the economy? Or are we actually picturing the economy as its own religion? I believe that neoliberalism and empire are their own kinds of religion that write in and protect certain kinds of religious expression and marginalize others. Christian religious practices, then, can reframe the moral universe and provide a trajectory and teleology that is not bound by stock market quarterly returns. I think religion can change time lines and imaginary possibilities. And in considering these questions, we should ponder how God might actually be present in all of this as well, that there is a way in which surprise and accountability and grace are present in these questions. What might an intentional meditation on this point look like, and what ways of seeing the world does God's revelation disrupt? I can't fully articulate this—I'm not a theologian by training—but there is something about meditating on the otherness of God that begs the question of whether there are other ways to see reality.

TOJ: Can you elaborate more on what it might look like to conceive of the church as offering a different framework without conceiving of it as a counterpolis? When we think of evil, we often think in terms of dichotomies—black/white, good/bad, sacred/profane. I'm curious about the connection between these two points—on the one hand, what it might mean to think about the imaginative possibilities enabled by and in religious communities without conceiving of the church as a distinct entity and, on the other hand, the contestation of dichotomies that religious activism offers?[4]

CMS: I don't think there are pure institutions or pure institutional practices, and I don't think that's the point. I do think, however, that there is a way in which the traditions of institutional community offer a primary stance that helps that community gain some critical distance on the multiple traditions which are present and talking to each other. There is a way in which every institution that we are in is part of the political economy—we are never capable of separating our institutional selves. This is a belief I share with Stanley Hauerwas and others: I believe deeply in the social self, and I cannot divide off, at any moment, my other formations. I am shaped by my formation as an athlete, by my formation in the academy, and by my formation in the US capitalist economy. There are ways, however, in which I can lean into certain institutional identities and meditate on them, ways that I can get some sense of the multiplicity of who I am. And that is actually my hope for what religious communities can do, through Sabbaths, rituals, and stories that repeat themselves. Those of us who use the lectionary tell the same stories in three-year cycles, and doing this

---

4. For more on the ways that ritual can play a helpful role in contesting sacred/profane and how it works politically, see chapter five, "Where Two or Three Are Gathered: Ritualizing Moral Agency," in *All You That Labor*, 122–40.

raises the question, how do we hear the formation of who we are again, anew? What I'm wanting from the church, then, and what I think is so important about religious communities, is an intentional space and time for the retrieval and remaking of those rituals which help us lean into the purposes and desires of God, a space and time where we consider the purposes of our lives and what redemption looks like in this world. Having an intentional time for such meditations doesn't mean that those communities avoid being formed around many of the same trajectories of a political economy, but I believe that intentionality toward asking certain kinds of questions is important.

There are so many activists in the living wage movement that have developed these remarkable rituals, some of which I tell about in the book, but to give one example—there is something about a minister visiting a restaurant in Los Angeles that's not giving contracts to its employees and standing up in her clergy collar and doing a five-minute homily in the restaurant about the workers serving there and then, at the end of that homily, leaving a tip for the people who served her coffee and having those employees applaud as she leaves and having the diners stunned because they have to think about what it means for them to think theologically about that space. So I'm deeply appreciative of the lessons that I've learned from colleagues in the movement who reclaim spaces about which many others would say, "No, no, no, the economy has no moral grounds and there is no divine action happening here." I think the reclaiming of these spaces as spaces of divine reflection and activity is incredibly powerful and deeply threatening on all sorts of levels.

It's remarkable which religious messages we allow into seemingly secular spaces and which ones we won't, which rituals are OK in "secular" spaces and which are not. And so the living wage movement, Occupy Wall Street, and other similar movements should be asking why we can't occupy work with religious sensibilities about what it means to have wholeness and redemption in relationships. That kind of reclamation of seemingly secular space by a different set of religious concepts is really important in the contestation that's happening right now.

TOJ: In *All You That Labor*, you situate the problems of low-wage workers within the contemporary context of neoliberal economics, highlighting many of its flaws and limits. Thinking a bit more about how the living wage movement is trying to address these kinds of issues within the context of late modernity, could you talk about how you see evil functioning and how you see it being named and resisted in relation to the current political and economic landscape? How do you see religious communities conforming to and resisting the current evils in our context?

CMS: This is a fascinating question in that I usually don't meditate on the category of evil. When I do think about it theologically, I conceive of evil as a deformation of the good. In moments like these, I'm struck by how Augustinian I am, but I think there is a way in which most theological thinking about neoliberalism is a bit Manichaean, something I think a lot of people, including many of my sheroes in feminist economic ethics, fall prey to. I think that we have to pay attention to how much our economic ideals around flourishing, freedom, and sustainability have drifted away from the good. When I think about the good, I think about Augustine's relational framework where the good is found in relationship to God and proper ordering of relationship to others. And there is a way in which evil is a deprivation of relationship and relational accountability. Evil no longer sees a face; it no longer has compassion; there are no longer bodies involved.

I will not completely write off neoliberalism. I think that there are some possibilities of social equity within neoliberalism. I have colleagues who would disagree strongly with that, but I also have a bit of realism in me about how economic systems work, and I believe it's important to think about how things can work within systems while still criticizing those systems. There is certainly a way in which neoliberalism becomes evil, when the relational moves into abstraction, when life becomes solely about the numbers on a page of quarterly earnings and those numbers no longer have any flesh attached to them. I think that Judith Butler partly points to this when she talks in the first issue of *Tidal* about embodiment in Occupy Wall Street.[5]

I think this attention to embodiment is present also in the living wage movement, where the workers are saying, "We have faces. We have bones that creak. We need, in all sorts of ways, attention to how we are actually physically present." This call is an invitation to move back toward the good and to resist evil. Faith communities cannot let abstraction be the owner of the narrative or the power; we need to see relationality and accountabilities. And this can be done in simple ways.

At a recent meeting of hotel workers, someone asked, "How can I be involved? How can I be present? I'm staying at a boycotted hotel, what do I do?" And there are very simple things a person can do: speak to the management; put all your towels up, which lessens the chance of repetitive strain injuries for your hotel worker; and leave notes about not needing things changed. All of that sounds trivial, and it is trivial. But it's important in terms of bringing faces, bodies, and joints back into our everyday encounters with the economy. And I think it is extraordinarily difficult to attend to these concerns, but that's actually one of the strengths of religious communities: they encourage us to attend to these narratives, make present voices that it would be easier

---

5. Butler, "For and Against Precarity," *Tidal: A Journal of Theory and Strategy for the Occupy Movement* 1 (December 2011): 12–13.

to leave out, and recognize that we are no longer whole when they're not in our moral imagination.

There is a way in which current economies disappear bodies. I was reading the feminist theologian Darby Ray the other day—she has this great little book *Working*—and she talks about the Fordist approach to the industrial revolution and how in post-Fordism we've seen a shift to an intellectual economy, a process in which we've lost the craftsperson and the people who are involved in production. It's not just the disappearance of work: it's the disappearance of working bodies. I think about that as I sit here in my office at a major academic institution—we have these odd categories for employees: there are workers, there are staff, and there are faculty. And our access to various parts of buildings is often defined by these categories; but where *are* the "workers" or lower-wage employees? Where are they allowed to go to the bathroom? What hallways are they allowed to go up? There's a great moment in the film *Bread and Roses* where custodians are scrubbing near the elevator, and people are just stepping over them, and the workers are talking about how they seem to have magical powers to just disappear. Alexia Salvatierra, the executive director of Clergy and Laity United for Economic Justice (CLUE) talks about how our job, their job, all of our jobs, is to make invisible people visible.[6] And I think that's a challenge in how we tell narratives, in how we get a kind of physical presence in an economy that relies on not seeing. Butler doesn't turn to religion for a number of reasons, but religion offers a space where these narratives can be told.

---

6. See Ray, *Working: Christian Explorations of Daily Living* (Minneapolis, MN: Fortress Press, 2011); *Bread and Roses*, directed by Ken Loach, released by Lions Gate Films. Also, note that CLUE is an organization of religious leaders in California that supports people's struggle for a living wage, health insurance, fair working conditions, and a voice in the decisions that affect them. Salvatierra speaks about these issues in Snarr, *All You That Labor*, 10 and Salvatierra, "Faith-Rooted Organizing: A New Response to the Age-Old Problem of Poverty," Pacific School of Religion, http://www.psr.edu/earl-lectures-2011-opening-worship.

17 Bloodline to Bethlehem: A Review of John Piper's *Bloodlines*

by BRIAN BANTUM

John Piper. *Bloodlines: Race, Cross, and the Christian*. Wheaton, IL: Crossway, 2011.

Bloodlines IS A CURIOUS book. In it John Piper, the prominent white pastor of Bethlehem Baptist Church in Minneapolis, Minnesota, steps out to speak about the problem of race in the American church. Where many prominent white clergy have remained silent, Piper turns his attention to one of the silent tragedies of American Christianity, the perpetual racial and ethnic division of its congregational life.

In so doing, Piper seems to be saying what many who are concerned with racial and ethnic division within the church have been hoping white Christians could say in these conversations. Piper first admits his own history of racism and bigotry (ch. 1), attending not only to the question of personal responsibility but also to the structural aspects of racism in the United States. Then, after highlighting Christ's own groundbreaking life—the ways in which his ministry continually broke through the racial and ethnic boundaries of his own time (ch. 7 and 8)—Piper concludes by calling Christians to mutual sacrifice at the cross of Christ, to never quit in our response to Christ's love and power, and to always seek harmony (ch. 16 and "Conclusion").

But *Bloodlines* is a curious book because lodged within these important contributions are approaches that seem to undercut the very aims Piper strives to articulate. For instance, Piper draws upon the work of such African American intellectuals as Michael Eric Dyson and Henry Louis Gates Jr. to highlight the realities of structural racism, but he compresses these conversations into three brief pages, whereas his discussion of racism and personal responsibility, leaning upon the work of such conservative African American intellectuals as Juan Williams, Shelby Steele, and Dinesh D'Souza, is much longer, is given more sympathetic treatment, and is drawn upon in various ways throughout the rest of the book. Piper claims to not take sides (85), and yet he leaves behind the insights of Dyson and Gates when it gets to the work of describing what "Christ-exalting" diversity looks like.

The way in which Piper navigates these various interlocutors suggests that within the vision of diversity that Piper imagines, the fundamental concerns of those contrary voices have only been faintly heard. Although he highlights Steele's exhortation that "What black and white Americans fear are the sacrifices and risks that true harmony demands" (233), Piper seems somewhat unwilling to allow conversation partners such as Dyson much say in his own vision of the world.

As Piper moves from a consideration of the social context of race to a consideration of how a Christian should understand these issues, he embarks upon an extended exegesis of Scripture, highlighting the ways in which Christ's life and work on the cross overcame ethnic division and provided a definitive answer to any notion of racial superiority. Piper's Christology, which is drawn from a neo-Reformed view, is aimed at showing that "not only did our ethnic distinctives contribute nothing to our election, and nothing to our ransom on the cross, but our ethnic distinctives also contributed nothing to the rise of our faith and the emergence of our repentance. We are all equally dependent on irresistible grace to be called and to believe and to be saved" (167).

Although few would argue that a Christocentric view isn't crucial to the church's wrestling with the question of race, Piper's emphasis on Christ's work and reconciliation transcends race and ethnicity in such a way that tends to erase Christ's personhood as a Jew. He undercuts his message of reconciliation and racial harmony by excising ethnic particularity from both our condition of unfaithfulness and our communion with God in heaven. Piper writes, "The seriousness of our sin is determined not mainly by the nature of our deed but the nature of the one we dishonor. A sin against an infinitely worthy God is an infinite sin. Color and ethnicity will count for nothing in the court of heaven. One thing will count: the perfection of Jesus Christ" (68). If this is the case, what is racial and ethnic difference at all? Is Christ no longer a Jew, and what does this mean for the lineage—or in Piper's words, the "bloodline"—of Israel? By making such claims, Piper strips away the significance of Christ's particular ethnic life and of our own racial, ethnic, and national lives. At best this fundamentally ignores Christ's participation in the liturgical and cultural life of Israel; at worst, it leans toward Gnosticism; and either way, by obscuring the particular characteristics of people, this kind of racial blindness runs counter to Piper's overarching goal of racial harmony.

Moreover, by potentially dismissing the specific demographic characteristics of Christ, Piper resists the complication of, as a Gentile, being grafted into another people. To trim off the fat of Christ's Jewish existence is to resist the deeply transformative implications of being knit into a new humanity. Here, the narrowness of Piper's interlocutors and theological grammar becomes problematically fused.

Within the last fifty years, many theologians—take for example Howard Thurman, James Cone, Virgilio Elizondo, Gustavo Gutierréz, Willie James Jennings, and J. Kameron Carter—have highlighted ways in which the separation of Christ from his Jewishness distorts a proper understanding of who Christ is and leads us to some of the most egregious contemporary betrayals of Christ's name, including the African slave trade and the perpetual anti-Semitism of the modern world. These theologians have demonstrated that such separations are not merely moments of blind unfaithfulness; they are profound misreadings of Christ's personhood, misreadings that draw believers into patterns of exclusion or coercive inclusion, which are often masked as practices of holiness or evangelism and missions. Piper attempts to narrate these misreadings as an example of humanity's pride. It is this pride, according to Piper, that is punished upon the cross, thus freeing us to enter into a just standing with Christ. But reducing pride to an abstract spiritual state is to lose the subtle ways that pride becomes manifest in our lives as a racially bound righteousness, a desire to see ourselves apart from one another. Pride is not simply an abstract consequence of the fall; it has a particular cultural and social shape.

Perhaps Piper is familiar with the work of these theologians, but if he is, there is little evidence of this in his account of Christ's work. There is little evidence here of Howard Thurman's observations regarding Christ's context as an oppressed Jew, Shawn Copeland's recent discussions of black female bodies as a way of understanding Christ's suffering, or Virgilio Elizondo's discussion of Christ's hybrid cultural position in Galilee. And the consequences of these gaps are clear. Piper's Christ is a raceless God-man, focused intently on a violent sacrifice that achieves the salvation of our souls with the happy consequence of taking our bodies along for the ride. Hence, the relationship between our bodies—our racial and ethnic particularity—and our salvation seems always to be at odds within Piper's theological framework. Sadly, Piper does not attend to the writings of black, womanist, or liberation theologians for whom the reality of difference, as it was forced upon them, is always a theological dilemma. Such an oversight is not simply a matter of insufficient research: it highlights the ways Piper has refused to engage in dialogue with different communities as he attempts to imagine what racial harmony could look like. The issue is not that Piper doesn't agree with the important voices who have a stake in these questions; the issue is that he makes no effort for *sincere* dialogue with these voices. Piper wants harmony within *his* view of Christ and the world.

The view of harmony Piper has in mind can be seen most clearly in how he tries to instill racial harmony in his own congregation. He provides impressive details concerning the steps his own congregation has taken to attend to questions of racial and ethnic diversity and social concerns. For instance, Piper initiated a revision of his church's mission statement to emphasize the centrality of God's work in the world in relationship to ethnic and racial diversity. One such initiative reads, "we will embrace the supremacy of God's love to take new steps personally and corporately toward racial reconciliation expressed visibly in our community and in our church" (260). In addition to revising its mission statement, Bethlehem has hosted conferences, created a Racial Harmony Task Force, and sought to encourage conversations about racial competency within their congregation and within their hiring processes. Piper outlines a tremendous commitment individually and institutionally to the question and reality of racial difference. In the midst of these endeavors, one might expect to see a thriving diverse pastoral leadership on Bethlehem Baptist Church's staff web page (of course, we will only see males in leadership positions, but that is a different article), but out of twenty pastors, *three* are non-white, and two of these non-white pastors are in urban- or ethnic-specific ministries. Put next to Piper's admission that he barely knows the diverse people of his church's local neighborhood (39), there arise certain questions about what Piper even means by racial harmony. What is the relationship between Piper and the diverse peoples of his neighborhood and how he seeks pastoral leadership in his own church?

Piper's narration of the ways in which the church frames the issue of diversity is particularly helpful in understanding why his staff remains so homogenous despite his commitment to the cause. Resisting the temptation to make diversity an issue that rules all others, Piper explains that the "nonnegotiables" which are operative when his church seeks a new pastor and elder are above all characterized by "a spirit of life and ministry captured by phrases such as God-centered, Christ-exalting, and Bible-saturated" (259). Of course, these seemingly benign descriptors have very specific political and theological content that resonate with Piper and Bethlehem's vision of the world.

Ultimately, these nonnegotiables display the limits to what Bethlehem and Piper are willing to imagine as God-centered diversity. Put differently, these qualifiers outline which differences are acceptable and which differences are unacceptable. Such differences are, however, only "doctrinal"—they lack any deep challenge on the grounds of race to a staff that is overly represented by white men. The consequence is that Piper is willing to advocate for diversity, but the boundaries of what this diversity might mean are so narrow that only varying shades of *his* theological vision are represented. Piper wants blacks and Latinos on his staff, but only those blacks and Latinos who think like him. But is this truly reconciliation? Is this harmony?

I'm not so sure. And to be fair, it seems Piper isn't always so sure either. He is willing to make mistakes and remain committed to a vision of a diverse, reconciled Christian community, but while he is to be commended for this, we must wrestle with the possibility that some roads are more dangerous than others, that our intentions are not always sufficient, and that sometimes it is not merely important *that* we come to the table but *how* we come to the table. And it is the *how* in *Bloodlines* that is difficult and curious. Piper declares the name of Christ in a way that silences all and that flattens the textures and particularities of human sinfulness. By wanting so desperately to emphasize black and white sinfulness as fundamentally the same, Piper forgets the powerful history of white men dictating and spiritualizing black "sinfulness." Although the state of alienation between humanity and God is certainly universal, the texture of how that sinfulness works over and against one another is not the same. The presumption of a white man naming the sin of black people is not new, even if Piper names the sin of white people too. In fact, such generalizations are part of the problem. The reality of sin draws us into patterns of life that are separate and in many instances contentious. But there are varied reasons for this and we all participate in varied ways. Piper's approach simply does not allow for these complications.

Piper narrates the power of Christ's work in a way that fundamentally erases ethnic or racial difference and yet he wants us to imagine diversity as important. He claims to desire racial harmony, and yet he displays no attention to how others have interpreted or been encountered by the Word made flesh. Piper wants to contribute to the conversation, and yet he has not attended to the conversation that has already been taking place among other folks for many, many years. Because of this, his plea for mutual confession and his proclamation of Christ do not instill hope in me. Instead, I fear that he will not hear those who do not sing in his key, those who do not echo back to him his convictions.

When we take seriously the life of Christ and the lives of Christians of different races and ethnicities, we are led into the dangerous possibility that we will end up more like "them" than they will look like "us." Such a possibility is encapsulated in Christ's own life; Christ was one who (to quote a different reformed theologian, Karl Barth) "did not will to be God without us" and whose very life now bears the mark of ethnicity, of a particular body.[1] For Christians concerned with the legacy of whiteness in the United States, it is no longer sufficient to simply begin with confession and hope to move quickly to Christ, past all the messy particularities of how we participate in this present state of unfaithfulness. What Piper fails to understand is that in preaching Christ, we open ourselves to a dangerous possibility: that *we* may have to change. To preach Christ means that some of our time-honored traditions,

---

1. See Barth, *Church Dogmatics*, vol. 4, pt. 1 (Grand Rapids, MI: William B. Eerdmans, 1981), 274.

the beliefs that we had concerning who God was and who we are, will be challenged when we are confronted with the God who, in a patriarchal society and within a religious tradition that was convinced God was forever hidden, at once made a woman into a priestess and her womb the Holy of Holies. God does some surprising things. There is no reconciliation without this fact. And yet it is this reality of God-with-us that modernity so fervently refused when a conception of whiteness, under the guise of Christ, was hurled upon the world. It is this reality we have yet to come to grips with, a reality that perpetually reiterates notions of faithful community within sameness. If Piper is sincere in his desire for a diverse community, perhaps he would do well to begin with a different confession, that his Jesus is not the only Jesus, that we all must bring our own confessions and our own stories to the table. I fear that in this book Piper is telling me what to bring to the table, how it will be prepared, and what the meal will look like when all is said and done.

In these many ways Piper's *Bloodlines* is a curious book. It is full of contradictions and good intentions, but ultimately it represents a conversational path that can only lead one place: to the doors of Bethlehem Baptist Church.

For readers who are looking for ways to rethink the church's role in racial reconciliation, there are many places that would provide excellent beginnings. Books that are more accessible include: Shawn Copeland's *Enfleshing Freedom: Body, Race, Being* (Minneapolis, MN: Fortress, 2010); Brenda Salter McNeil's *A Credible Witness* (Downers Grove, IL: InterVarsity 2008); and Curtiss Paul De Young's *United By Faith* (New York, NY: Oxford University Press, 2003). For more scholarly engagements with questions of church, race, and ethnicity, see James Cone's *God of the Oppressed* (Maryknoll, NY: Orbis, 1997); Gustavo Gutiérrez's *On Job* (Maryknoll, NY: Orbis, 1997); Willie James Jennings's *The Christian Imagination* (New Haven, CT: Yale University Press, 2010); and J. Kameron Carter's *Race: A Theological Account* (New York, NY: Oxford University Press, 2008).

18 A Sense of Place: Flannery O'Connor and the Local Church

by ANDREW W. E. CARLSON

THE WHOLE SOUTH WALL of my home seemed ready to collapse under a distressed drumming at the door one recent evening. While my wife went to the peephole I recollected some words from a sermon I'd heard years ago: "If our church catches on to the radical extent that Jesus calls us to love our neighbors, we'll be the sort of community that has prostitutes banging down the doors." When I first heard that challenge I don't think I took it quite this literally.

I am part of a faith community called Awake Church, which has bound itself to a particular location along part of Seattle's iconic Aurora Avenue. My church-planting pastor, Ben, had the seemingly simple idea when he began putting together our faith community that our mission would be to undertake Jesus's command to "love your neighbor," and we would do it in this particular place.

We could have picked a neighborhood where that's a little easier. This secularized city is full of charming places that would benefit from the attention of some youthfully optimistic church folks. Yet we ended up in the neighborhood of Aurora, a neighborhood that is generally characterized by its less alluring attributes: seedy motels, vacant lots, various abused chemicals, sexual promiscuity, and the like. The land along this old highway is an eyesore, a blemish in Seattle's otherwise clear complexion, and everyone seems to be sneering, "Can anything good come from Aurora?"[1]

But I have been digging, trying to unearth signs of Grace, and I have been discovering Jesus on Aurora in the same way that I have learned to recognize the incarnation in Flannery O'Connor's fictional worlds. O'Connor was driven by an artistic impulse to discover moments of grace as penetrations in the darker parts of reality, and rather than blinding us with beautiful images of redemption—in which

---

1. See John 1:46.

she resolutely believed—she challenged her readers to find life in places where it's harder to see. Reading her work, I sometimes get the sense that she was putting God to the test by contending so boldly what others do blithely, that if the incarnation of God in Jesus Christ is somehow an animation of *all* reality, then in even the worst of our human predicaments we should be able to find signs of Grace. Aurora appears to be one of those darker places, and our church has been engaging in a provocation of O'Connor's sort by pushing hard into that reality.

Jesus mingled with the socially demoralized, living alongside them in their present state of reality. The challenge of our work, which centers itself on that story of incarnation, is that we have to learn how to balance the neighborhood *as it is* with our hope for the way things one day *will become*. Our church community has found that committing to remain in this tension between those two ways of seeing the world is surprisingly radical. It deviates from the well-intentioned imperialist dreams of those who wish to drive out the "problems" in order to, as representatives of the city would say, "revitalize Aurora." But one of the first things Ben clarified when he got this community in motion is that we are not out to impose our view of what a redeemed Aurora should look like, rather we're attempting to discover that redemption together with our neighbors. Ben says we are searching for the marks of incarnation in Aurora under the assumption that, despite the general public's perceptions, "a faithful and loving God is already at work. We simply wake up to what the Spirit is already doing."[2]

This is what I mean by comparing our work to O'Connor's storytelling. She reproaches novelists who "try to shake off the clutches of their region" in order to write a story with a more universal appeal. Her work is distinctively Southern, and she claimed that such a careful attentiveness to place is the only way to write decent fiction. O'Connor says, "The discovery of being bound through the senses to a particular society and a particular history, to particular sounds and a particular idiom, is for the writer the beginning of a recognition that first puts his work into real human perspective."[3] Her own work was an attempt to dig deep into her Southern soil and then trust that stirring things up might somehow persuade Grace to emerge there, in the reality of her place.

The first time my wife and I decided to check out Awake Church, there was a gathering taking place on a Sunday evening in the backroom of a coffee shop called the Sweet Spot. We walked around the building to a narrow concrete stairway leading

2. Ben Kat, "Aurora Part III," *Awake the Dawn*, September 28, 2007, http://awakeseattle.blogspot.com/2007_09_01_archive.html.

3. O'Connor, *Mystery and Manners: Occasional Prose*, ed. Robert and Sally Fitzgerald (New York, NY: Farrar, Straus and Giroux, 1969), 198.

down to a door that one might have thought required a specific knock. I felt like we were persecuted Christians gathering in secret 100 years in the future or 1800 years in the past. Everyone had brought food to share, potluck style, and we wandered through the assembled crowd until Ben called us all together.

"Welcome, Awake," he said—I noticed it was not, "Welcome *to* Awake"—"I just got word that one of the motels down the street has been condemned by the city for health code violations. It's getting shut down and everyone who has been staying there is required to move out tonight. So right now, for our worship time, we're going to take a walk over to give those folks a hand."

The dozen or so of us headed up the street. When we arrived, I was shocked to realize that these were more than seedy motel rooms; these were people's homes. I met one elderly woman who had been living there for nearly twenty-five years. And there was very little we could do other than to be present, which gave me an immediate taste of what it meant to be part of Awake, to be willing to hang around in the middle of social untidiness.

A few months after that first experience with Awake, my wife and I discovered an apartment for rent in a fourplex across the street from that still-condemned motel. We moved there because they would take our dog and because it was fairly inexpensive. But it has felt like a rite of passage into a new way of being, like a comprehensive identification with Awake's neighbor-loving mission. We could not have known then the profound impact that would come to us and our community from simply living day to day in that space, cultivating a place of hospitality, and allowing ourselves to be shaped by our neighborhood.

The apartment came with a large but miserably unloved backyard. But in a concrete jungle, the little patch of weeds had the rare potential to be a botanical haven. So the members of the Awake community started putting their imaginations together to consider how the yard might be put to use in a way that would cultivate our mission, that would allow us to, as O'Connor put it, "penetrate the surface of reality," and to do it quite literally.[4] We started harrowing the soil and plucking out used IV needles, keys, condoms, and shards of broken glass. People from the neighborhood took notice of the work going on back there and began to join in on the effort, building garden boxes, relandscaping, planting, watering, and then watching the new life emerge. The outcome was a genuinely communal garden.

One Wednesday evening we had a celebratory cookout in the garden that attracted many of the people who were wandering by and it helped us discover that the people in our church community weren't the only ones looking for ways to connect with neighbors. And so we began hosting the cookouts more frequently, and they have now become a regular Wednesday evening occurrence during the summer

---

4. Ibid., 168.

months, a weekly time of connecting. I have been amazed at the way people from every walk of life are so happily willing to wander across social barriers into these momentary experiences of an alternative reality.

There used to be a coffee shop next door to our garden that was named A Better Buzz (a nod to the local Alcoholics Anonymous fellowship). The coffee shop went out of business a couple of years ago and our church has taken over the lease. Over the past year, we all worked together to do a large-scale remodeling project, turning the space into something that I like to describe as a neighborhood living room. We have named it the Aurora Commons. The Commons provides the safety of hospitality so that our neighborly interactions can flourish. It feels to me like an extension of the garden's mystery, only with a roof to enable year-round access to that mystery.

Ben found out not long after naming our church "Awake" that in Latin *Aurora* means "dawn." The Psalmist says, "My heart is steadfast, O God, my heart is steadfast! . . . I will awake the dawn!" (Psalm 57:7–8 NRSV). Our church began with the intention to love our neighbors and we are right now living in the middle of that story, trying to be attentive to the moments of Grace as they emerge. We have few presumptions for what that should look like, and we're uncertain about what it will become, but the act of binding ourselves to unlovable Aurora has enabled us to see further into the great reach of the incarnation.

And I've started to wonder if these moments of Grace are becoming easier for us to see because we are now more connected to the stories that redemption comes wrapped up in. I'm thinking, for instance, of my neighbor Denny who sleeps in an old conversion van on my street. A year ago Denny was nearly suicidal in his depression. He and I have spent a great deal of time working through this together, but no matter how hard Denny tried, he could not escape the world he was living in twenty years ago, when he was a drummer in a grunge rock band. Our church has struggled deeply with him, too, and on his behalf tried to imagine what something like redemption might look like for him now. It has seemed always to no good end, and I have quite often found myself on the edge of giving up hope for him.

That is really the question of all our work. How do we imagine redemption? And how do we set aside our preconceptions in order to see what it will look like? The appearance of redemption is God's to determine, and if we try to initiate it without a story, without a sense of place, we may be making a frightfully imperialist advancement. It seems to me the best we can do is keep on digging and overturning soil until some sign of Grace finally emerges within our field of view.

It is enough that the other night I saw Denny camped out next to a bonfire in the garden because, he said, "I felt like lying under the stars."

O'Connor says, "The novel that fails is a novel in which there is no sense of place." In response to a handful of manuscripts she reviewed, she criticized the language and characters because they seemed like they had emerged out of a television. Despite the fact that these writers all lived in the South, O'Connor said, "[Their characters] might have originated in some synthetic place that could have been anywhere or nowhere." I think you can easily read "church communities" in place of "stories" in her grievance about writers who do not root their work in a particular place: "They want to write about problems, not people; or about abstract issues, not concrete situations." She says, "They don't have a story and they wouldn't be willing to write it if they did."[5]

A lot of people write stories with the idea of achieving some kind of universal appeal. It's no different with music, film, and poetry. And I think most of us know this happens with churches as well. Too often O'Connor's line is a fitting description for these churches: they could be located "anywhere or nowhere." And I think it is important to recognize the sentiments behind the seamless and captivating but utterly generic programs of such universally appealing churches. The disjointed but collaborative composition that makes up our neighborhood faith community's *ecclesia* is different because it is an unearthing of Grace that is bound up in the sense of place.

Awake gathers together in the Commons somewhat dependably every Sunday now. Denny has been playing a drum lately, which I don't think any of us could have imagined a year ago, and adding his voice to mine, and to my neighbors, and to the socially demoralized, and to the youthfully optimistic, as we together worship a God who breaks into all the corners of reality.

---

5. Ibid., 199, 56, and 90.

19 O for a Thousand Tongues to Mutter

by JENNIFER STRANGE

For a fallen soldier

Today, two gray ministers meet a body,
go before it, sing or say some pale business
about our utterly solitary passage in and out of life,

during which we may resolutely bless the Lord
and, after a while, simply resurrect.
Today, well-meaning ministers speak some truth

to a hollow congregation sick of death.
In a plain chapel with no more kneeling room,
the unpracticed will oblige and recite wisdom:

first "Let us count our days aright" and then
"Help us want your ever-present hope." But today
I'm in the woods, where the usual corruption

seems a little more corrupt than before:
ants smell and swarm a single worm,
a blue jay chases from her nest two black crows,

rattlesnakes follow a trodden path and hide to strike
when the trespasser recrosses his log.
And the red-cockaded woodpecker grays her longleaf,

releasing sap so rat snakes seeking her young
will crawl back down or else fall off,
retreat to the ancient groundcover, waiting for fire.

Contributors

Allison Backous is the creative writing editor for *The Other Journal*. She holds an MFA in creative nonfiction from Seattle Pacific University and teaches at Kuyper College in Grand Rapids, Michigan.

Brian Bantum is an assistant professor of theology at Seattle Pacific University and the author of *Redeeming Mulatto: A Theology of Race and Christian Hybridity* (Baylor University Press). He writes and teaches on the intersections of Christ, identity, and Christian life. Bantum lives in Seattle, Washington, with his wife, Gail Song Bantum, and his three children.

Richard Beck is a professor of psychology at Abilene Christian University and the author of *Unclean: Meditations on Purity, Hospitality, and Mortality* (Cascade). As an experimental psychologist, Beck has published extensively on the intersection of Christianity and psychology. He also writes regularly about the interface of theology and psychology at his popular and award-winning blog *Experimental Theology*.

Gregory A. Boyd is cofounder and senior pastor of Woodland Hills Church in Maplewood, Minnesota. For sixteen years, Boyd served as professor of theology at Bethel University in St. Paul, Minnesota, where he still teaches on occasion. He has authored or coauthored nineteen books, including *The Myth of a Christian Nation* (Zondervan) and *God at War* (InterVarsity). Boyd and his wife live in community with several other families in St. Paul and have three grown children, five grandchildren, and an adorable dog named Max.

Andrew W. E. Carlson lives in Seattle, Washington, with his wife, Lisa, and their baby daughter, Cedar Harrow. He is pastor of liturgy for Awake Church and a part-time carpenter. Carlson spends his free time climbing in the mountains, sitting by a fire with a novel, or sitting by a fire in the mountains. He is an MDiv graduate of the Seattle School of Theology and Psychology.

J. Kameron Carter is an associate professor in theology and black church studies at Duke Divinity School and a member of Duke University's graduate faculty on religion. His first book, *Race: A Theological Account* (Oxford University Press), was received widely as a major contribution to modern theological discourse. He is currently working on a book titled *The Secular Jesus: Political Theology from Columbus to the Age of Obama* (Yale University Press).

Brandy Daniels is a PhD student in theological studies and a fellow in the theology and practice program at Vanderbilt University. Her work explores the intersections of theology and critical gender and race theory, with particular emphases on Dietrich Bonhoeffer, Michel Foucault, and Judith Butler.

Mark Fleming lives in Greensboro, North Carolina, and teaches creative writing and storytelling at Guilford Technical Community College. His essay "Poses" appears in *Exiled—Voices of the Southern Baptist Convention Holy War* (University of Tennessee Press) and his story "A Father's Place" appears in the anthology *Surreal South '11* (Press 53). The former deacon chair of a not-your-mama's Baptist church, Fleming is seeking a publisher for his third novel, *The Nun, the Alien, and the Amish Boy: Gospels*.

Jacob H. Friesenhahn teaches theology at John Paul II Catholic High School in Schertz, Texas. He is the author of *The Trinity and Theodicy: The Trinitarian Theology of von Balthasar and the Problem of Evil* (Ashgate).

Chad Gusler has an MFA in creative writing from Seattle Pacific University. He teaches at Eastern Mennonite University in Harrisonburg, Virginia.

Richard Kearney holds the Charles Seelig Chair of Philosophy at Boston College and is a visiting professor at University College Dublin. He is the author of over twenty books on the philosophy of religion, art, and culture, including *The Wake of Imagination* (Century Hutchinson), *Poetics of Imagining* (HarperCollins), *On Stories* (Routledge), *Strangers, Gods and Monsters* (Routledge), *The God Who May Be* (Indiana University Press), and most recently, *Anatheism: Returning to God after God* (Columbia University Press).

Chris Keller is the founding editor of *The Other Journal* and a psychotherapist in Seattle, Washington.

David Kline holds an MLitt in Bible and the contemporary world from St. Andrews University and is currently a third-year MDiv student at Duke Divinity School. He attends the Emmaus Way church with his wife, Hannah, in Durham, North Carolina.

Ronald A. Kuipers is an associate professor in philosophy of religion at the Institute for Christian Studies in Toronto, Canada. He is the author of *Critical Faith: Toward a Renewed Understanding of Religious Life and its Public Accountability* (Rodopi) and is currently putting the finishing touches on a book-length introduction to the philosophy of Richard Rorty for Continuum Press's Contemporary American Thinkers series.

Agustín Maes has fiction appearing in *Blue Mesa Review*, *Gallatin Review*, *Turnrow*, *Ontario Review*, and *Albawtaka Review*. His work has been included in *New Stories from the South: The Year's Best, 2007*, cited as a distinguished mystery story by *The Best American Mystery Stories 2007*, and named one of two runners-up for the 2011 Paris Literary Prize. Maes holds an MFA in fiction writing from the New School in New York City and an MA in theology from the University of San Francisco. He was also a Milton Center Postgraduate Fellow at *Image* journal in Seattle, Washington.

Rebecca Martin lives with her husband and daughter in Virginia's Blue Ridge Mountains. She holds an MA in English literature from the University of Georgia, and her work has been included in the *Curator*, *Lamppost*, an edited collection of Narnia essays, and *Kinfolk Magazine* (forthcoming). She blogs about mountain drives, local produce, family, and books at www.rebarit.blogspot.com.

Branson Parler is an assistant professor of theological studies at Kuyper College in Grand Rapids, Michigan. He has published essays on John Howard Yoder in *Power and Practices: Engaging the Work of John Howard Yoder* (Herald) and *Radical Ecumenicity: Pursuing Unity and Continuity after John Howard Yoder* (Abilene Christian University Press). His forthcoming *Things Hold Together: John Howard Yoder's Trinitarian Theology of Culture* will be published by Herald in the fall of 2012.

Anthony B. Pinn is the Agnes Cullen Arnold Professor of Humanities and a professor of religious studies at Rice University in Houston, Texas. He is also the director of research at the Institute for Humanist Studies in Washington, DC.

Dan Rhodes is editor-in-chief of *The Other Journal*. He is also a minister of political and missional life at Emmaus Way in Durham, North Carolina, and the author (with Tim Conder) of *Free for All: Rediscovering the Bible in Community* (Baker Books). He is currently a theology PhD candidate at Duke University Divinity School. He lives in Raleigh, North Carolina with his wife, Elizabeth.

C. Melissa Snarr is the associate dean for academic affairs and an associate professor of ethics and society at Vanderbilt University Divinity School. Her work focuses on the intersection of religion, social change, and political ethics. The author of numerous articles and books, her most recent work, *All You That Labor* (New York University Press), explores the role of religious activists in the living wage movement.

Jennifer Strange has work appearing in *Oxford American*, *Christianity and Literature*, *Rock and Sling*, *The Southern Poetry Anthology*, and the *Art House America* blog, for which she serves as assistant editor. She taught at Centenary College of Louisiana and works as a freelance editor when she isn't baking for her husband, their two sons, and their ornery old cat.

Kali Wagner, a Tennessee transplant living in Seattle, Washington, recently graduated from Seattle Pacific University with degrees in English and reconciliation studies. She loves crypts and the word *Tallahassee*. This is her first published poem.

Lauren Wilford is an intern for *Image* journal and a film and music blogger. She studies aesthetics and narrative as an undergraduate at Seattle Pacific University.

Christian Wiman is the editor of *Poetry* magazine and the author of the poetry collections *The Long Home* (Story Line) and *Every Riven Thing* (Farrar, Straus and Giroux), as well as the essay collection *Ambition and Survival: Becoming a Poet* (Copper Canyon). His work has appeared in the *Harvard Divinity Bulletin*, *New Yorker*, *Harper's Magazine*, and *Atlantic*.

www.ingramcontent.com/pod-product-compliance
Lightning Source LLC
Chambersburg PA
CBHW080603170426
43196CB00017B/2892